THE FOUNDATION

OF

AUGUSTINIAN–CALVINISM

THE FOUNDATION OF AUGUSTINIAN–CALVINISM

Copyright © 2019 Regula Fidei Press

Printed in the United States of America

Library of Congress Cataloging-in-Publication Data

ISBN: 9781082800351

1. Augustinian–Calvinism 2. Stoicism
3. Neoplatonism 4. Gnostic 5. Manichaeism

For those persons who are not afraid

to allow truth to triumph over tradition

Preface

The title of this book expresses my intention to help people understand Calvinism's construction of that impressive systematic theology upon the foundation of Augustine's theology.

Augustinian-Calvinism is a self-designated term by Calvinists (Reformed theologians) who understand the Augustinian foundation of that theological building (as will be discussed later). I was asked to summarize my Oxford doctoral thesis in a brief and simplified form so other readers could understand the foundation of Augustinian-Calvinism.[1] This book answers that request regarding my doctoral thesis at the University of Oxford in 2012, entitled, "Augustine's Conversion from Traditional Free Choice to 'Non-free Free Will': A Comprehensive Methodology." For that project, I read all of Augustine's extant works, letters, and sermons chronologically and compared them with the various religious and philosophical beliefs on fate and free will from 2000 BCE to 400 CE, including the earlier Christian authors (early church fathers). That thesis underwent numerous corrections and material was added, including a subject index and a list of scriptures used by Gnostics and Manichaeans to prove their determinism. This was published as Kenneth M. Wilson, *Augustine's Conversion from Traditional Free Choice to "Non-free Free Will": A Comprehensive Methodology* in Studien

---

[1] This occurred after my video interview with Dr. Leighton Flowers was made public on February 26, 2019. Dr. Flowers is the Director of Evangelism and Apologetics for Texas Baptists and the host of the podcast "Soteriology 101." The video link of our February 26, 2019 interview is available at https://youtu.be/BnOMORGM2Qw.

Und Texte Zu Antike Und Christentum 111 (Tübingen: Mohr Siebeck, 2018). Both my book *Augustine's Conversion* and this book are written in a spirit of acceptance of differences between religious groups. Too many divisions already exist within every religion. Calvinism reaches back to Augustine's ideas and interpretations of scripture; but, does not understand the foundation of Augustine's determinism within earlier non-Christian philosophies and religions. Calvinists consistently write and speak of Augustine's doctrines as following the apostle Paul. This book will help reveal these other influences on Augustine's later deterministic theology.

This current book provides a very abbreviated and simplified access to the major concepts of my work.[2] This includes ancient philosophies and religions, the early Christian authors (95–400 CE), and the reasons for Augustine's theological and philosophical conversion from the unanimous voice of earlier Christian authors to his later novel theology. The quotations in foreign languages and ancient languages have been replaced with English translations. Complex material and vocabulary have been simplified for the non-scholar. Latin titles and references have been retained since translations often have different chapter numberings. The bibliography and appendices are not reproduced from my book *Augustine's Conversion*.

This abbreviated book is inadequate for critical evaluation in a scholarly study. Scholars who are interested in this topic and would like to read my full interaction with the primary source materials in the original languages and engage the complexities of the arguments should read and respond to the entire published scholarly work (ISBN-13: 978-3161557538, also available as an e-book from Mohr Siebeck). A critique or review of this simplified book by any scholar should not be considered a scholarly response unless he

---

[2] Credit and appreciation to Traci Emerson, J.D., M.L.I.S. for helping to accomplish this task. Whatever challenges remain for the reader are of my doing.

or she has previously publicly reviewed my complete scholarly book in a peer reviewed journal or book. I find it necessary to explicitly state this because many persons, even scholars, may be tempted to dismiss the conclusions for personal reasons and avoid (even subconsciously) legitimately researching Augustine's conversion to determinism.

Calvinists consistently write and speak of Augustine's doctrines as following the apostle Paul. This book will help reveal other important influences on Augustine's later deterministic theology. After considering these additional influences upon the Bishop of Hippo, persons may then decide whether these influences were too extensive to accept Calvinism or whether they will continue to believe the great Augustine was in agreement with the apostle Paul. My hope is that each reader will carefully consider the evidence presented in this book and will engage with questions of Christian free will and determinism with an open mind.

Table of Contents

Abbreviations

General Abbreviations

1 Apol. and 2 Apol.	*Apology 1 and Apology 2*	Justin Martyr
Ad Marc.	*Ad Marcellam*	Porphyry
Adv. def. orig. pecc.	*Adversus defendendum originale peccatum*	Theodore
Adv. haer. / AH	*Adversus haeresis*	Irenaeus
Adv. Mac. spir. sancto	*Adversus Macedonianos de spiritu sancto*	Gregory
Adv. Marc.	*Adversus Marcionum (Against Marcion)*	Tertullian
An.	*De anima*	Tertullian
AugStud	*Augustinian Studies*	
Autol.	*Ad Autolycum*	Theophilus
Barn.	*Epistle of Barnabas*	
Cat.	*Catecheses*	Cyril of Jerusalem
Cat. mag.	*Oratio catechetica magna*	Gregory
CCL	*Corpus christianorum series latina*	
CMC	*Cologne Mani-Codex*	
Comm. Ev. Jo.	*Commentarii in evangelium Iohannis*	Origen
Comm. Ioh.	*Commentarium Iohannan*	Theodore
Comm. Romanos	*Commentariorum in Romanos*	Ambrosiaster

Comm. Rom.	*Commentarii Romanos*	Origen
C. Ar.	*Contra Arianos*	Athanasius
C. Eun.	*Contra Eunomium*	Gregory
Cels.	*Contra Celsus*	Origen
Corp. Herm.	*Corpus Hermeticum*	Gnostic
Cult. fem.	*De cultu feminarum*	Tertullian
CSEL	*Corpus scriptorum ecclesiasticorum latinorum*	
DH	*Definitions of Hermes Trismegistus to Asclepius*	Gnostic
De Abrah.	*De Abraham*	Ambrose
De bapt.	*De baptismo*	Tertullian
De cib. Jud.	*De cibis Judaicis*	Novatian
De prov.	*De providentia*	Alexander of Aphrodisias
De resurr.	*De resurrectione*	Athenagoras
Dial.	*Dialogue with Trypho*	Justin Martyr
Dial. de anima et res.	*De anima et resurrectione dialogus*	Gregory
Diogn.	*Epistle of Diognetus*	
Disc.	*Discourses*	Epictetus
Div.	*De divinatione*	Cicero
DUPIED	*Divine Unilateral Predetermination of Individuals' Eternal Destines*	
Enn.	*Enneads*	Plotinus
Ep. (ep.)	*Epistle*	
Exc. Satyri	*De excessu fratris sui Satyri*	Ambrose
Exc. Theod.	*Excerpta ex Theodoto*	Theodotus the Valentinian

Fat.	*De fato*	Cicero
Haer.	*Refutatio omnium haeresium*	Hippolytus
Hom. Hex.	*Homilae Hexaēmeros*	Basil
Hom. Psa.	*Tractatus super Psalmos*	Hilary
Inst.	*Divinarum institutionum*	Lactantius
JECS	*Journal of Early Christian Studies*	
M.	*Mani*	Cologne Mani Codex
Mir. M.	*Mitteliranishce Manichaica*	
Opif. hom.	*De opificio hominis*	Gregory
PG	*Patrologia graeca*	
PL	*Patrologia latina*	
PLS	*Patrologia Latina Supplementum*	
P. Arch.	*Peri Archon*	Origen
P.P.	*Peri pascha*	Melito
Paen.	*De paenitentia*	Ambrose
Praep. ev.	*Praeparatio evangelica*	Eusebius
Princ.	*De principiis*	Origen
Ref. conf. Eun.	*Refutatio confessionis Eunomii*	Gregory
Sent.	*Sententiae ad intelligibilia ducentes*	Porphyry
S. Q. Hoarti Flacci	*Sermomum Quinti Horatii Flacci poëmata*	Horace
Sir.	*Sirach*	
ST	*Summa theologica*	Thomas Aquinas
St.Patr.	*Studia patristica*	
Strom.	*Stromata*	Clement
Symp.	*Symposium decem virginum*	Methodius
Treat.	*Treatise*	Cyprian

Treat. Res.	*Treatise on the Resurrection*	Gnostic
Val.	*Adversus Valentinianos*	Tertullian
Vig.Chr.	*Vigiliae Christianae*	

Tanakh (Christian Old Testament)

Gen.	Genesis
Exod.	Exodus
Lev.	Leviticus
Deut.	Deuteronomy
Josh.	Joshua
1 Sam.	1 Samuel
1 Kgs.	1 Kings
Ps.	Psalms
Prov.	Proverbs
Eccl.	Ecclesiastes
Isa.	Isaiah
Jer.	Jeremiah
Ezek.	Ezekiel

New Testament

Matt.	Matthew
Rom.	Romans
1 Cor.	1 Corinthians
2 Cor.	2 Corinthians
Gal.	Galatians
Eph.	Ephesians
Phil.	Philippians

1 Thess.	1 Thessalonians
1 Tim.	1 Timothy
2 Tim.	2 Timothy
Phlm.	Philemon
Heb.	Hebrews
Jas.	James
1 Pet.	1 Peter
2 Pet.	2 Peter

Works by Augustine of Hippo

Acad.	*Contra Academicos (Against the Academics)*
Adim.	*Contra Adimantum (Against Adimantus)*
Agon.	*De agone christiano (The Christian Struggle)*
Bapt.	*De baptismo contra Donatistas (On Baptism Against the Donatists)*
Bon. conj.	*De bono coniugali (On the Good of Marriage)*
Catech. rud.	*De catechizandis rudibus (Instructing the Unlearned)*
Civ.	*De civitate dei (City of God)*
Conf.	*Confessiones (Confessions)*
C. Adim.	*Contra Adimantum (Against Adimantus)*
C. du. ep. Pel.	*Contra duas epistulas Pelagianorum (Against the Two Letters of the Pelagians)*
C. Jul.	*Contra Iulianum (Against Julian)*
C. litt. Petil.	*Contra litteras Petiliani (Against the Letters of Petilian)*
Corrept.	*De correptione et gratia (On Rebuke and Grace)*
Div. quaest.	*De diversis quaestionibus octoginta tribus (On eighty-three different questions)*
Doctr. chr.	*De doctrina christiana (Christian Doctrine)*

Enchir.	*Enchiridion ad Laurentium de fide spe et caritate (Enchiridion)*
Exp. prop. Rom.	*Expositio quarumdam quaestionum in epistula ad Romanos (Exposition on questions in the Epistle to the Romans)*
Faust.	*Contra Faustum (Against Faustus)*
Fel.	*Contra Felicem Manichaeum (Against Felix the Manichaean)*
Fid. op.	*De fide et operibus (On Faith and Works)*
Fid. symb.	*De fide et symbol (Faith and the Creed)*
Fort.	*Contra Fortunatum Manichaeum (Against Fortunatus the Manichaean)*
Gen. litt.	*De Genesi ad litteram (Literal Commentary on Genesis)*
Grat. Chr.	*De gratia Christi et de peccato originali (The Grace of Christ and Original Sin)*
Grat.	*De gratia et libero arbitrio (Grace and Free Will)*
Immort. an.	*De immortalitate animae (Immortality of the Soul)*
Leg. adv.	*Contra adversarium legis et prophetarum (Against the Adversaries of the Law and Prophets)*
Lib. arb.	*De libero arbitrio voluntatis (On Free Will)*
Nat. bon.	*De natura boni contra Manichaeos (The Nature of the Good Against the Manichaeans)*
Nat. grat.	*De natura et gratia (On Nature and Grace)*
Nat. orig.	*De natura et origine animae (On the Nature and Origin of the Soul)*
Ord.	*De ordine (On Providence)*
Pecc. merit.	*De peccatorum meritis et remissione et de baptismo parvulorum (On the Forgiveness of Sins and the Baptism of Infants)*
Persev.	*De dono perseverantiae (The Gift of Perseverance)*
Praed.	*De praedestinatione sanctorum (On Predestination of the Saints)*
Quant. an.	*De animae quantitate (The Measure of the Soul)*
Retract.	*Retractationes (Retractions)*

S.	*Sermones (Sermons)*
Simpl.	*Diversis quaestionibus ad Simplicianum (Various Questions to Simplician)*
Solil.	*Soliloquia (Soliloquies)*
Spir. et litt.	*De spiritu et littera (On the Spirit and the Letter)*
Symb.	*De symbolo ad catechumenos (The Creed to the Unlearned)*
Trin.	*De trinitate (The Trinity)*
Unit. eccl.	*Ad Catholicos epistola contra Donatistas vulgo de unitate ecclesiae (To the Catholics: On the Unity of the Church Against the Donatists)*
Ver. rel.	*De vera religione (On True Religion)*

Translations and Citations

The primary sources for quotations in Greek and Latin in my original doctoral thesis and *Augustine's Conversion* were *Patrologia Graeca*, *Patrologia
Latina*, *Corpus Christianorum Series Latina*, and *Corpus Scriptorum Eccle-
siasticorum Latinorum*. Unless otherwise indicated and when translations
exist in the series, all English translations of Augustine's works are derived
from *The Works of Saint Augustine: A Translation for the 21st Century* from
the Augustinian Heritage Institute, Inc. and published by New City Press,
Hyde Park, New York (1990–2018). Scriptural citations in English are from
the Revised Standard Version and English Standard Version. Translations
into English from modern languages in this short book are my own and also
from ancient languages unless otherwise stated in my book *Augustine's Conversion*.

Introduction

Although it may appear to be an impressively constructed building, a systematic theology is only as good as its foundation. Protestant Reformed theology in the sixteenth century was built on Augustine's foundation through Martin Luther (an Augustinian monk) and Calvin (an ardent disciple of Augustine). The prestige of Augustine as a theologian-philosopher may be unsurpassed in Western Christianity, yet Eastern Christianity does not revere him.[3] He is not a father of the Eastern Orthodox Church as he is in Roman Catholic Church, nor does Eastern Christianity quote him as an important authority as occurs in Protestant writings. This book explores Augustine's conversion from the traditional Christian view of free choice in salvation (battling Stoic and Gnostic determinism) back to his prior Manichaean view of divine unilateral determinism of eternal destinies (heaven or hell).

Within Christianity, theological truth is not primarily measured by its antiquity, but by its conformity to scripture, logic, and then with a consideration of tradition. The 500-year-old theology of John Calvin was directly derived from Augustine who strayed from the foundation of traditional patristic theology over a thousand years prior to Calvin. We need to explore the novel foundation on which Augustine laid his later Christian theology. This will expose the fact that Augustinian-Calvinism's

---

[3] Michael Azkoul, *The Influence of Augustine of Hippo on the Orthodox Church* in Text and Studies in Religion, vol. 56 (Lewiston, NY: Edwin Mellen, 1990), 33–42 and iii: "There is good reason that Orthodoxy [Greek/Russian] has never recognized him as a Father of the Church."

impressively logical skyscraper has been built upon an unstable foundation of pagan syncretistic (mixing pagan and Christian ideas) sand.

Augustine of Hippo's early influences from Stoicism, Neoplatonism, and Manichaeism ultimately determined his final theology, with his later deterministic interpretations of scripture reverting to his pre-Christian Manichaean interpretations. The key scriptures cited in modern defenses of Reformed theology are the very ones used by the heretical Manichaeans in the fourth and fifth centuries and imported into Christianity by Augustine. Numerous scholars cite these scriptures and cite Augustine as proof for the validity of their Augustinian-Calvinist interpretations. They remain unaware of the pagan Stoic, Neoplatonic, and Manichaean origins of these highly deterministic interpretations of scripture.

Augustine invented the five points of Calvinism that comprise TULIP: Total depravity, Unconditional election, Limited Atonement, Irresistible grace, and Perseverance of the saints. The most important of these was total depravity (with human loss of free will resulting in total inability to respond to God). This then required unconditional election (God unilaterally must give the gift of faith) and perseverance of the saints (since God's gifts are perfect). Irresistible grace and limited atonement were logical deductions from the three major doctrinal shifts. This resulted in the self-designated term "Augustinian-Calvinism" by theologian Paul Helm.[4] Helm is correct since Calvin admitted, "Augustine is so wholly within me that I could write my entire theology out of his writings."[5]

---

[4] Paul Helm, *"The Augustinian-Calvinist View"* in James Bielby and Paul Eddy, eds. *Divine Foreknowledge: Four Views (Downers Grove, IL: IVP), 161–189.*

[5] John Calvin, "A Treatise on the Eternal Predestination of God," in John Calvin, *Calvin's Calvinism*, trans. Henry Cole (London: Sovereign Grace Union; repr., 1927), 38. Calvin in his *Institutes* quotes Augustine many hundreds of times.

Therefore, we will first briefly examine the teachings of Stoicism, Neoplatonism, Gnosticism, and Manichaeism. Next, the writings of Christian authors (early Christian fathers) prior to Augustine's conversion will be explained in their battle against these pagan deterministic philosophies (the study of the early Christian fathers is called Patristics). Finally, we will thereafter research Augustine's early traditional Christian views, and then explore when and why he converted to his later deterministic views.

The more one understands Stoicism, Neoplatonism, and Gnostic Manichaeism, and the more one has read Augustine, the more Augustine's dependence upon his prior philosophies and religion in his 412 CE conversion to deterministic "non-free free will" becomes apparent. The facts do not support the popular claim that reading scripture (Romans, Galatians, and 1 Corinthians) was the impetus for Augustine's deterministic conversion in his alleged (but erroneously dated) 396 CE work *Ad Simplicianum* 2.

A comprehensive chronological (in the order they were written) reading of all of Augustine's works, sermons, and letters provides the only way to comprehend what happened to the famous bishop of Hippo; and therefore, what happened within Western Christianity. Because of Augustine, many Protestants in the Reformation eagerly embraced theological determinism as a Christian concept.

> For whoever reads my works in the order in which they were written will perhaps discover out how I have made progress over the course of my writing.
> –Augustine (*Retract.*, Prol.3).

Chapter 1
Stoicism, Neoplatonism, Gnosticism, and Manichaeism

Scholars have identified Stoicism, Neoplatonism, and Gnostic Manichaeism as important influences on Augustine of Hippo.[1] He spent years personally involved in these three extremely deterministic philosophies. The terms fate and predestination carry considerable philosophical and theological connotations. Therefore, I coined the phrase Divine Unilateral Predetermination of Individuals' Eternal Destines (DUPIED) to explore the similarities and differences between pagan and Christian literature without importing biased concepts.[2]

---

[1] John Rist, *Stoic Philosophy* (Cambridge: Cambridge University Press, 1969); Marianne Djuth, "Stoicism and Augustine's Doctrine of Human Freedom after 396" in Joseph C. Schnaubelt and Frederick Van Fleteren, eds. *Augustine: Second Founder of the Faith.* Collectanea Augustiniana (New York: Peter Lang, 1990); Gerard O'Daly, *Platonism Pagan and Christian: Studies in Plotinus and Augustine* (Aldershot, UK: Ashgate, 2001); Johannes Van Oort (2006). "Augustine and Manichaeism: New Discoveries, New Perspectives," *Verbum et Ecclesia JRG* 27.2 (2006): 710–728; N. Joseph Torchia, "St. Augustine's treatment of superbia and its Plotinian Affinities," *Aug.Stud.* 18 (1987): 66–79; M. Testard, *Saint Augustin et Cicerón*, Bd.1: Cicerón dans la formation et dans l'œuvre de saint Augustin; Bd. 2 : Répertoire des textes (Paris, 1958).

[2] Hereinafter the phrase "Divine Unilateral Predetermination of Individuals' Eternal Destines" will be used interchangeably with its acronym DUPIED.

A. Stoicism

The first deterministic influence on Augustine was Stoicism, which taught every miniscule event in the universe was controlled by fate. The Stoic philosopher Seneca the Younger stated it succinctly, "The fates lead the willing and drag the unwilling."[3] A human had to be totally virtuous or totally corrupt without any middle ground. In Stoicism, only the wise person was free.[4]

Stoics taught a "non-free free will" to solve what they perceived as a problem with the human "evil willer/chooser." Humans were captives to bad choices because their innate choosing ability was faulty. The Stoic Chrysippus (*ca.*279–*ca.*206 BCE) had cleverly redefined causal determinism (everything is caused). He separated it from necessity (fate) through utilizing a counterfactual possibility of impossible opportunity. In other words, even though a person had zero possibility of not following his or her fate, the opportunity still existed and therefore "free will" remained (*Fat.*12–15).[5] This could be compared to a pre-programmed robot choosing what was programmed when given an opportunity of "choice." Chrysippus also alleged a compatibility (both can be true simultaneously) between this strict determinism and "free will" by creating the idea of an infinite regress (going backwards in time to prior causes an infinite number of times).[6] But even

---

[3] Lucius Seneca, Epistle to Lucilius.

[4] Bertrand Russell, *A History of Western Philosophy* (London: George Allen and Unwin, 1946.; repr., London: Routledge, 2004), 253–254; Rist (1969), 24–27.

[5] Anthony A. Long and David N. Sedley, *The Hellenistic Philosophers*, vol.1 (Cambridge: Cambridge University Press, 1987), 393.

[6] Philosophically this is a disingenuous (not recognized as a legitimate) argument.

this regress itself was ambiguous in respect to what this term 'caused' could mean.[7] In Chrysippus' teaching, human actions are caused/fated because:

1.) Our character is caused/fated from external influences upon us.

2.) Our character causes/fates our assent (what we decide), and therefore

3.) our moral culpability exists because we assent (agree/decide).

Thus Chrysippus demands moral culpability for a person *despite* him or her being controlled by fated assent from fated character due to fated external causes. That means Stoicism's strict determinism was hidden within a mere facade of "free will." This facade was "non-free free will" (fated free will)— an oxymoron.[8] The analogy Stoics used was a dog tied by a rope to a horse-drawn cart. The dog has free will: the dog may choose to follow the cart or be dragged by the cart. Despite this analogy, scholars have correctly assessed the Stoic's 'relative free will' within their determinism as not allowing free choice.[9] Stoic determinism cannot be reconciled with a genuine free choice. As a result, "The Stoics faced a serious challenge in their attempt to reconcile moral responsibility with determinism" which they tried to evade by rhetorically redefining assent: the "internal cause which is the locus of responsibility is assent," and viewed assent as "an unfailing cause of impulses."[10] The Stoics' conclusion? Assent (agreement/choices) itself was fated. Like some modern philosophers and theologians, Stoics side-stepped the incompatibility of determinism and free choice by redefining terms and inventing clever

---

[7] Brad Inwood, *Ethics and Human Action in Early Stoicism* (Oxford: Clarendon Press, 1985), 69–70.

[8] An oxymoron is a term that contradicts itself and cannot be true.

[9] David Winston, "Chapter 13: Philo of Alexandria," in Lloyd P. Gerson, ed. *The Cambridge History of Philosophy in Late Antiquity* (Cambridge: Cambridge University Press, 2010), 248, fnt.13.

[10] Inwood (1985), 45–55.

nuances. Despite their nuances, Stoics believed every event in the universe was pre-determined and fated by the gods.

Augustine's first work, *On Providence* (*De ordine*, 386 CE) teaches this Stoic philosophy when asserting that the falling of a leaf to an exact location is predetermined by a meticulous micromanaging God and the precise neck muscle actions of two roosters fighting are predetermined by God.[11] Augustine himself singled out (Stoic) Providence as the one belief he never doubted throughout his diverse philosophical-religious journeys (*Conf.*6.5,7; cf. *Ord.*2.12).

B. Neoplatonism

Augustine's second influence for determinism was Neoplatonism, instituted by Plotinus (*ca.*250) and popularized by Porphyry (*ca.*350). Plotinus rejected the Jewish and Christian view that humanity retained the *imago Dei* (divine image) after the first human's fall into sin. That divine image was totally lost when the immaterial soul became connected with physical matter and that divine image could only return at death when physical matter (the body) is removed (*Enn.*1.1.12; 4.3.12).[12] The goal of life is "bringing back the god in oneself to the divine in the all" by reabsorption into the One (*Enn.*1.4; 3.7.34.19, similar to "the Force" in Star Wars that does not possess a

---

[11] Augustine, *De providentia*, 1.12–25.

[12] Kevin Corrigan, *Reading Plotinus: A Practical Introduction to Neoplatonism* (West Lafayette, IN: Purdue University Press, 2005), 46–47; Mark Edwards, *Neo-platonic Saints: The Lives of Plotinus and Proclus by Their Students.* Translated with an introduction (Liverpool: Liverpool University Press, 2000), xxviii.

personality).[13] Plotinus borrowed Aristotle's distinction that only the soul freed from the body could be free to reason correctly; and therefore, a person in a body cannot have free will (*De provid.*3.1.8).[14]

Evil does not come directly from being physical matter (as it does in Gnosticism/Manichaeism) but the combination of matter, soul, and body introduces evil.[15] Freedom for a person's soul cannot occur without direct association with the Intellect or One Soul (*Enn.*4.3.5.15).[16] Plotinus thought he had reconciled apparent contradictions between necessity and free choice. Humanity's voluntary free choice, to become physical rather than remain purely spiritual, destroyed free choice. Therefore, free choice must be restored by a divine infusion to restore the will (*Enn.*3.2.9.1, 2.3.1.1, 3.3.19–21; 4.8.5.1– 4). Citing *Enn.*4.4.44.32, scholar Georges Leroux emphasizes that in this system all persons involuntarily commit evil, yet all are still morally culpable for their sin.[17]

Despite teaching this Stoic view of strict unilateral divine determinism, both Plotinus (*Enn.*2.9.1–3; 3.9.3; 5.1.2) and Porphyry (*Ad Marc.*24; *Sent.* 31; *Praep. ev.* 11.28.15) are typically treated in modern works as teaching

---

[13] A.P. Bos, "World-views in Collision," in David T. Runia, ed. *Plotinus amid Gnostics and Christians* (Amsterdam: Free University Press, 1984), 13. "[H]e formulates man's task as 'bringing back the god in oneself to the divine in the all.'"

[14] Cf., Carlos Steel, *Proclus:* On Providence (London: Duckworth, 2007), 6–7; Cf. *De provid.*15 on *De anima* 1.1, 403a 10–12 and *De provid.*56–57 and 63.

[15] Denis O'Brien, "La matière chez Plotin: son origine, sa nature," *Phronesis* 44.1 (1999): 45–71.

[16] Georges Leroux, "Human Freedom in the Thought of Plotinus," in Lloyd P. Gerson, ed. *The Cambridge Companion to Plotinus* (Cambridge: Cambridge University Press, 1996), 298; similar to the Stoic's proverb that only the wise person is free.

[17] Leroux (1996), 311.

free will instead of determinism. Why?—Because they defined determinism as referring *only* to astrology. As long as one did not appeal to the stars as controlling human destinies then it was not classified as deterministic fate. This *theoretically* preserved αὐτεξούσιον (autexousion, what depends upon us humans), but still demanded a strict determinism since divine beings control humans in every aspect of life (Stoic Providence). The All-Soul must give the gift of love to individuals' souls. This comes by the Spirit who implants the desired love (*Enn.*3.5.4; cf., 1.7.9). This divine infusion is required because 'the will' (Stoic "willer")[18] has been bound by innate universal wickedness (*Enn.*3.2.10). Evil produced a totally incapacitating fall, imprisoning us against our wills and creating an "evil willer" (*Enn.*1.8.5). Thus, paradoxically, souls have neither genuine free will nor act by compulsion (*Enn.* 4.3.13). Humans are free to choose only what our totally corrupted 'willer' desires (again, borrowed from Stoicism).

The Neoplatonic "Reason-Principle" (god) desired and created more evil persons than good. This god created evil persons and predestined them to damnation devoid of human choice, but humans remain inexcusably culpable and guilty. Why? Because, the universe is just and good when every person plays his divinely assigned part, even those tortured humans screaming from Tartarus (*Enn.*3.2.17).[19] "The One" (god) can only choose and do good and thereby is exonerated by fiat of any injustice. Like the Stoics, Plotinus

---

[18] Despite millennia of philosophical adherence to a human faculty of "willer" (part of the human body that causes us to desire or choose), modern medicine nor science nor the Bible know anything of a faculty that causes humans to "will." See my forthcoming book, *God's Sovereignty: An Historical, Philosophical, and Theological Analysis*, 2020.

[19] Long and Sedley (1987), 342, 392. Tartarus is the place of punishment for wicked dead.

attempts to convince us that the possibility of a contrary desire or alternative action need not be present for something to be voluntary, but is a product of "non-free free will" (*Enn*.6.8.3–4). For these reasons, scholars (and other persons familiar with Augustine's writings) recognize Augustine was heavily influenced by the pagan deterministic writings of Plotinus, Porphyry, and Cicero.[20]

C. Gnosticism

The essential element in order to be categorized as a 'Gnostic' is the belief that a rival evil god created the evil cosmos composed of physical matter.[21] Gnostics were cosmic dualists, meaning that everything composed of physical matter was evil and everything non-physical (spiritual) was good. Humans are born evil because they possess a physical body. Therefore humans are damned at birth. Valentinus, a Gnostic, taught God offered the message of salvation to every human equally; however, only the predetermined elect were empowered by god to accept that invitation.[22] The Gnostic god unilaterally restored right reason to the helplessly corrupted human will through a

---

[20] Gerard O'Daly, *Platonism Pagan and Christian: Studies in Plotinus and Augustine* (Variorum Collected Studies Series 719, Farnham, UK: Ashgate, 2001) and Augustine Curley, O.S.B. "Cicero, Marcus Tullius," in Allan D. Fitzgerald, ed. *Augustine Through the Ages: An Encyclopedia*. Grand Rapids, MI: Eerdmans, 1999), 190–3.

[21] Mark Edwards, *Catholicity and Heresy in the Early Church* (Farnham: Ashgate, 2009), 1; found in Porphyry's title to *Enn*.2.9.

[22] Albrecht Dihle, *The Theory of Will in Classical Antiquity* (Berkeley, CA: University of California Press, 1982), 151–154; *Ev. Ver*.11, 30–31; *Corp. Herm*.1.26. The elect were πνευματικοί (spiritual ones) possessing Light particles required for salvation from ignorance.

gift to the mind (*Corp. Herm.*4.4; 6,68.36; 6,69.31–32; DH.5.3). When divine grace implanted that spiritual seed then the elects' salvation was compelled by their new "free will" by their own "free choice." The scholar Gilles Quispel articulated this Gnostic Valentinian separation of the elect ("predestined not to fall into foolishness") from the damned evil nature of the majority of humanity (*Treat. Res.*46).[23] "All works are predestined, discipline and abstinence effect nothing, and the elect are saved by knowing that they are saved."[24]

In contrast, the ὑλικοί (persons of earthly matter) were hopelessly damned from birth.[25] The Gnostic portrayal of Pharaoh as a ruined nature incapable of salvation precipitated Origen's famous rebuttal (*Princ.*3.1.8) in defending free choice against Gnostic Divine Unilateral Predetermination of Individuals' Eternal Destinies (DUPIED). Several Gnostic texts in the Nag Hammadi Library describe God's *command* to be saved or God's sole prerogative to save only some. This is a DUPIED requirement.

> It is God's business to save whom he wants; it is the business of the god-loving man to beseech God to save everyone. (*Sentences of Sextus* [Pythagorean], 373–374)

When the Gnostic god gave (forced) what he commanded, then he could command whatever he willed (humans would obey without fail).

---

[23] Gilles Quispel. "The Original Doctrine of Valentine," *VC* 1 (1947): 43–73.

[24] Mark Edwards, *Culture and Philosophy in the Age of Plotinus* (London: Duckworth, 2006), 152.

[25] King doubts Irenaeus' credibility; Karen King, *What is Gnosticism?* (Cambridge: Belknap Press of Harvard University Press, 2003), 205; but see Wilson, *Augustine's Conversion*, 13–15.

Present a command to us to see Thee, so that we may be saved. Knowledge of Thee, it is the salvation of us all! Present a command! When Thou dost command, we have been saved. (*The Three Steles of Seth*, 125; cf. *The Teaching of Silvanus*, 114–115).[26]

"Only because the supreme God, in His infinite mercifulness and inscrutable will, at a certain moment decided to turn Himself towards the potential Gnostic, can he effectively convert himself."[27] The Gnostic god must regenerate a person before that person is able to believe. Also in Gnosticism both 'free will' and 'forced grace' are taught simultaneously. Unfortunately, only the elect were given a healed 'free will' to accept this salvation offered to "everyone" (but offered unequally, cf. Hippolytus, *Haer.*5.14.1).

Jewish, Christian, and pagan philosophers alike unanimously denounced Gnostic Divine Unilateral Predetermination of Individuals' Eternal Destinies (DUPIED) because it robbed humans of free choice, self-determination, and the universal opportunity for salvation.[28] Irenaeus of Lyons (*ca.*180) argued against Gnostic determinism, comparing their view to Stoic determinism (*Adv. haer.*1.6.2; 2.29.1–31; 2.14.4).[29] Clement of Alexandria refuted the Gnostic Basilides' followers who claimed faith itself was a gift of God, with some persons being incapable of belief because they did not receive that

---

[26] Note the similarity between this phrase from the Gnostic *The Three Steles of Seth* and Augustine's famous line in his *Confessions* 10.31 to which Pelagius reacted as being a non-Christian concept: "Oh Lord, command what you will and give what you command."

[27] Giovanni Filoramo, "The Transformation of the Inner Self in Gnostic and Hermetic Texts," in Jan Assmann and Guy G Stroumsa, eds. *Transformations of the Inner Self in Ancient Religions* (Leiden: Brill, 1999), 139.

[28] Dihle (1982), 152.

[29] Jens Holzhausen, "Valentinus and Valentinians," in Wouter Hanegraaff, ed. *Dictionary of Gnosis and Western Esotericism,* vol.2 (Leiden: Brill, 2005), 1150–1154; cf. Origen's *Comm. Ev. Jo.*, fr.46 (John 8:44a).

'natural' gift of faith (*Strom*.2.3–4). Clement claimed Gnostics used scripture (such as Romans 11) to prove their determinism (*Exc. Theod.* 56.3–27).[30] The premier church historian, Chadwick, summarized the early Christian response to Gnosticism:

> For in rejecting the Gnostic way the Christians thereby rejected as inauthentic adulteration and corruption any theology of pure revelation teaching salvation by an arbitrary predestination of the elect and the total depravity of the lost, and possessing no criteria of rational judgment.[31]

D. Manichaeism

Augustine's third deterministic influence was Manichaeism, which evolved from Gnosticism as its greatest child. Manichaeism was also dualistic—the physical body was evil and the spirit was good. To birth a child was sin. Persons were unilaterally pre-determined before birth by the good god (who did not create physical matter) to be either elect or damned independently of human choice—again, Divine Unilateral Pre-determinism of Individuals' Eternal Destinies (DUPIED). In Manichaeism, the 'enslaved will' cannot choose—it is damned until unilaterally released by "reconciliation to God through Christ."[32]

In Manichaeism, Primeval Man (the first human) used free will to abandon his position in the realm of light and went down into matter and darkness.

---

[30] Jeffrey Bingham, "Irenaeus Reads Romans 8: Resurrection and Renovation," in Kathy Gaca and Laurence Welborn, eds. *Early Patristic Readings of Romans* in Romans Through History and Culture Series (London: T & T Clark, 2005), 124.

[31] Henry Chadwick, *Early Christian Thought and the Classical Tradition* (Oxford: Clarendon Press, 1966), 9.

[32] Caroline Hammond Bammel, „Manichaeism," in *Der Römerbrieftext des Rufin und seine Origenes-Übersetzung*, AGLB 10. (Freiburg im Breisgau: Herder, 1985), 7.

Escape then became impossible. The Manichaean doctrine of cosmic origins relies enormously on sexual lust among the gods/archons (rulers), called "the seduction of the archons."[33] Mani invented Manichaeism to be a syncretistic (a combined) religion for all persons worldwide by combining Judaism and Buddhism, then adding Christianity. His views on sex originated with his Elchasaite sect that prohibited sexual intercourse even within marriage. Sex was evil. Even the innate human desire for sex (concupiscence) was sin. He held the theory that sexual passion during human intercourse transmits sin itself to the children.[34]

Mani also borrowed the concept of humanity's total inability to respond to God from the ancient Indo-Mesopotamian *Maitrāyana Upanishad* IV. This work describes humans as robbed of freedom, imprisoned, drugged by delusion, and in deepest darkness. "He awakens Adam from the sleep of death, shakes him, opens his eyes, raises him up, exorcises demons to free him of demon possession, shows him all of imprisoned [physical] matter and suffering light soul."[35]

---

[33] Johannes van Oort, "Manichaeism," in Wouter Hanegraaf, ed. *Dictionary of Gnosis and Western Esotericism*, vol.2 (Leiden: Brill, 2005), 757–765.

[34] Johannes van Oort, "Augustine and Mani on concupiscentia sexualis," in J. den Boeft and J. van Oort, eds. *Augustinina Traiectina. Communications présentées au Colloque International d'Utrecht*, Paris: Études augustiniennes, 1987), 137–152; van Oort, "Augustine on sexual concupiscence and original sin," *StPatr* 22 (1989): 382–386.

[35] Geo Widengren, *Der Manichäismus* (Darmstadt: Wissenschaftliche Buchgesellschaft, Abt.,1977), 63–65; My translation of his „Alle diese Bilder kehren im Manichäismus wieder, 'Erweckt er Adam vom Schlafe des Todes, schüttelt ihn, öffnet seine Augen, richtet ihn auf, befreit ihn durch Exorzismus von den Dämonen, von denen er besessen ist, zeigt ihm die in der ganzen Materie gefangene und leidende Lichtseele.' "

The Redeemer commands (an awakening from drunken slumber) and then gives what he commanded by granting grace (in order to gaze upon deity): "The Redeemer, the just Zoroaster, spake thus with his soul: 'Deep is the drunkenness in which thou slumberest, awake and gaze upon me! Grace upon thee from the world of peace whence for thy sake I am sent.'" (M.7.82–118, Mir. M. III, p.27). Like both Neoplatonism and Gnosticism, Manichaeism requires the divine being to unilaterally awaken a "dead soul" who only then can respond to the divine being.

Like Plotinus taught, Manichaeism also taught free will was totally lost after humanity's fall. Because of this total depravity, Manichaean salvation emphasizes Christ's grace that dominates many prayers and hymns. For example, one Manichaean prayer requests Jesus to "Come with Grace" eleven times (M.2.28).[36] One scholar aptly summarized the response of the philosopher Alexander of Lycopolis to Manichaean 'grace:' "Alexander is shocked by Manichaean limitation of the path to salvation to the elect. For him, this directly contradicts the idea of a Providence, by definition equally caring for all."[37]

The theologian Christopher Hall notes, "Manichees assimilated to the religions around them, resembling Buddhists in the East and looking like a

---

[36] Widengren (1977), 90. „Dann folgt das Hauptstück, das in einem Gebet um die Epihanie besteht: Komm mit Heil!" cf. English Translation, *Mani and Manichaeism* (1965), 86–88.

[37] Gedaliahu Stroumsa, "Titus of Bostra and Alexander of Lycopolis: A Christian and a Platonic Refutation of Manichaean Dualism," in Richard T. Wallis, ed. *Neoplatonism and Gnosticism* (New York, NY: State University of New York Press, 1992), 344.

Christian sect in the West."[38] Augustine spent ten years as a Manichaean, participating as a "hearer."[39] As we will discover, many of his later doctrines can be traced to this deliberately syncretistic philosophy.

E. Conclusion

Stoic Providence apparently created similarities in Neoplatonism, Gnosticism, Manichaeism, and even the Jewish Qumranites through the concept of a divine unilateral meticulous providence (Divine Unilateral Predetermination of Individuals' Eternal Destinies).[40] All of these:

1.) require divine micromanagement causing even the smallest details occurring within the cosmic order (in modern terms called specific sovereignty),

2.) substitute the Jewish and Christian residual *imago Dei* for a view of humanity as worthless worms completely undeserving of God's attention or care as Creator

3.) teach humanity's 'free will' (specifically the ability to make choices for good) was destroyed or died, rendering it impossible for a person to even make a request for divine assistance,

4.) teach God must resurrect "dead wills/persons" by a unilateral infusion of grace, faith, and/or love,

---

[38] Christopher Hall, *Learning Theology with the Church Fathers* (Downers Grove, IL: InterVarsity Press, 2002), 195.

[39] Henry Chadwick, *Augustine: A Very Short Introduction* (Oxford: Oxford University Press, 1986), 14. A hearer was a disciple attempting to be one of the elect. Chadwick proved it was ten years, not the commonly accepted nine years of time Augustine was a Manichaean.

[40] For Qumranic determinism, see Wilson, *Augustine's Conversion*, 23–28.

5.) conclude it is true (as a result of the preceding assumptions) that mi-cromanaging Providence must utilize Divine Unilateral Predetermina-tion of Individuals' Eternal Destinies in choosing the elect and damned.

Augustine of Hippo was trained in Stoicism and embraced it even after becoming a Christian. He credits his own conversion to Christianity as oc-curring through the philosophy of Neoplatonism.[41] Augustine spent ten years of his early life in the Manichaean sect. Although he taught Christianity's traditional general sovereignty with free choice prior to 412 CE, this changed to Stoic/Neoplatonic/Gnostic-Manichaean determinism thereafter. As we will learn in the next chapter, no extant Christian author prior to Augustine taught anything other than genuine free choice in combating the rigid deter-minism of these pagan philosophies.[42]

---

[41] *Conf.* 7:9–16.

[42] For an overview of the various early Jewish perspectives see Wilson, *Au-gustine's Conversion*, 19–32.

Chapter 2
Early Christian Authors 95–400 CE

Early Christian authors unanimously taught *relational* divine eternal predetermination. God elected persons to salvation based upon foreknowledge of
their faith (predestination). These Christians vigorously opposed the *unilateral* determinism of Stoic Providence, Gnosticism, and Manichaeism.[1] So
early Christians taught predestination,[2] but refuted Divine Unilateral Predetermination of Individuals' Eternal Destinies (unilateral determinism). This
unilateral determinism can be identified in ancient Iranian religion, then
chronologically in the Qumranites, Gnosticism, Neoplatonism, and Manichaeism. "Christian" heretics such as Basilides who taught God unilaterally
bestowed the gift of faith to only some persons (and withheld that salvific
gift to others) were condemned. Of the eighty-four pre-Augustinian authors
studied from 95–430 CE, over fifty addressed this topic. All of these early

---

[1] Sarah Stroumsa and Guy. G. Stroumsa, "Anti-Manichaean Polemics in Late Antiquity and under Early Islam," *HTR* 81 (1988): 48.

[2] Wallace wrongly claims, "In spite of the numerous New Testament references
to predestination, patristic writers, especially the Greek fathers, tended to ignore the
theme before Augustine of Hippo. This was probably partly the result of the early
church's struggle with the fatalistic determinism of the Gnostics"; Dewey Wallace,
Jr. "Free Will and Predestination: An Overview," in Lindsay Jones, ed. *The Encyclopedia of Religion*. 2nd edn., vol.5. (Farmington Hills, MI: Macmillan Reference
USA, 2005), 3203. He obviously had not read Irenaeus and other early authors. For
a cogent refutation of this absurd claim, see in the same volume C.T. McIntire
(2005), "Free Will and Predestination: Christian Concepts," vol.5, 3207.

Christian authors championed traditional free choice and relational predestination against pagan and heretical Divine Unilateral Predetermination of Individuals' Eternal Destinies.[3]

This can only be understood and appreciated by reading comprehensively
through the sizeable number of works by these authors. Some persons trium-
phantly cite ancient Christian authors claiming they believe Augustine's deterministic interpretations of scripture, *but without* reading the entire context
or without understanding the way in which words were being used.[4] I am not
aware of any Patristics (early church fathers) scholar who would or could
make a claim that even one Christian author prior to Augustine taught Divine
Unilateral Predetermination of Individuals' Eternal Destinies (DUPIED, i.e.,
non-relational determinism unrelated to foreknowledge of human choices).

A. Apostolic Fathers and Apologists 95–180 CE

Most of these works do not directly address God's sovereignty or free will.[5]
The *Epistle of Barnabas* (100–120 CE) admits the corruption of human nature (*Barn*.16.7) but only physical death (not spiritual) results from Adam's
fall. Personal sins cause a wicked heart (*Barn*.12.5). Divine foreknowledge
of human choices allowed the Jews to make choices and remain within God's
plan, resulting in their own self-determination (*Barn*.3.6). God's justice is
connected with human responsibility (*Barn*.5.4). Therefore, God's

---

[3] Wilson, *Augustine's Conversion*, Appendix III, 307–309.

[4] Wilson, *Augustine's Conversion*, 41–94, and see other comments in the work
revealing how this occurs.

[5] For *The Shepherd of Hermas* and other works not covered here see Wilson, *Augustine's Conversion*, 41–50.

foreknowledge of human choices should affect God's actions regarding salvation.

In *The Epistle of Diognetus* (120–170 CE) God does not compel anyone. Instead, God foreknows choices by which he correspondingly chooses his responses to humans. Meecham writes of *Diogn.* 10.1–11.8, "Free-will is implied in his capacity to become 'a new man' (ii,I), and in God's attitude of appeal rather than compulsion (vii, 4)."[6] Aristides (*ca.* 125–170 CE) taught newborns enter the world without sin or guilt: only personal sin incurs punishment.[7]

I.   Justin Martyr and Tatian

The first author to write more specifically on divine sovereignty and human free will is Justin Martyr (*ca.* 155 CE). Erwin Goodenough explained:

> Justin everywhere is positive in his assertion that the results of the struggle are fairly to be imputed to the blame of each individual. The Stoic determinism he indignantly rejects. Unless man is himself responsible for his ethical conduct, the entire ethical scheme of the universe collapses, and with it the very existence of God himself.[8]

Commenting on *Dial.* 140.4 and 141.2, Barnard concurred, saying God "foreknows everything—not because events are necessary, nor because he has decreed that men shall act as they do or be what they are; but foreseeing all events he ordains reward or punishment accordingly."[9] After considering 1

---

[6] Henry Meecham, *The Epistle to Diognetus: The Greek Text* (Manchester: Manchester University Press, 1949), 29–30.

[7] Harold Forshey, "The doctrine of the fall and original sin in the second century," *Restoration Quarterly* 3 (1959): 1122, "But in this instance the doctrinal presupposition shows through clearly—a child comes into the world with a *tabula rasa.*"

[8] Erwin Goodenough, *The Theology of Justin Martyr* (Jena: Verlag Frommannsche Buchhandlung, 1923), 219.

[9] Leslie Barnard, *Justin Martyr: His Life and Thought* (Cambridge: Cambridge University Press, 1967), 78.

*Apol.*28 and 43, Chadwick also agreed. "Justin's insistence on freedom and responsibility as God's gift to man and his criticism of Stoic fatalism and of all moral relativism are so frequently repeated that it is safe to assume that here he saw a distinctively Christian emphasis requiring special stress."[10] Similarly, Barnard wrote: "Justin, in spite of his failure to grasp the corporate nature of sin, was no Pelagian blindly believing in man's innate power to elevate himself. All was due, he says, to the Incarnation of the Son of God."[11]

Tatian (*ca.*165) taught that free choice for good was available to every person. "Since all men have free will, all men therefore have the potential to turn to God to achieve salvation."[12] This remains true even though Adam's fall enslaved humans to sin (*Or.*11.2). The fall is reversed through a personal choice to receive God's gift in Christ (*Or.*15.4). Free choice was the basis of God's rewards and punishments for both angels and humans (*Or.*7.1–2).

II. *Theophilus, Athenagoras, and Melito*

For Theophilus (*ca.*180), all creation sinned in Adam and received the punishment of physical decay, not eternal death or total inability (*Autol.*2.17). Theophilus' insistence upon a free choice response to God (*Autol.*2.27) occurs following his longer discussion of the primeval state in the Garden and subsequent fall of Adam. Christianity's gracious God provides even fallen Adam with opportunity for repentance and confession (*Autol.*2.26). Theophilus exhorts Christians to overcome sin through their residual free choice (*Autol.*1.2, 1.7).

Athenagoras (*ca.*170 CE) believed infants were innocent and therefore

---

[10] Henry Chadwick, "Justin Martyr's Defence of Christianity," *Bulletin of the John Rylands Library* 47.2 (1965): 284; cf., 291–292.

[11] Barnard (1967), 156.

[12] Emily Hunt, *Christianity in the Second Century: The Case of Tatian* (New York, NY: Routledge, 2003), 49.

could not be judged and used them as a proof for a bodily resurrection prior to judgment (*De resurr.*14). For God's punishment to be just, free choice stands paramount. Why?—because God created both angels and persons with free choice for the purpose of assuming responsibility for their own actions (*De resurr.*24.4–5)[13] Humans and angels can live virtuously or viciously: "This, says Athenagoras, is a matter of free choice, a free will given the creature by the creator."[14] Without free choice, the punishment or rewarding of both humans and angels would be unjust.

In *Peri Pascha* 326–388, Melito (*ca.*175 CE) possibly surpassed any extant Christian author in an extended description depicting the devastation of Adam's fall.[15] The scholar Lynn Cohick explained: "The homilist leaves no doubt in the reader's mind that humans have degenerated from a pristine state in the garden of Eden, where they were morally innocent, to a level of complete and utter perversion."[16] Despite this profound depravity, all persons remain capable of believing in Christ through their own God-given free choice. No special grace is needed. A cause and effect relationship exists

---

[13] Bernard Pouderon, *Athénagore d'Athènes, philosophie chrétien* (Paris: Beauchesne, 1989), 177–178. Pouderon highlighted this requisite for God's law and justice: "La liberté humaine se tire de la notion de responsabilité: 'L'homme est responsable (ὑπόδικος) en tant qu'ensemble, de toutes ses actions' (*D.R.*XVIII, 4)." "Human freedom results from the concept of responsibility: 'Man is generally responsible (ὑπόδικος) for all his actions.'" (my translation)

[14] David Rankin, *Athenagoras: Philosopher and Theologian*. Surrey: Ashgate, 2009), 180.

[15] Stuart Hall, *Melito of Sardis: On Pascha and Fragments* in Henry Chadwick, ed. Oxford Early Christian Texts (Oxford: Oxford University Press, 1978), xvi, where *The Petition To Antonius* "is now universally regarded as inauthentic."

[16] Lynn Cohick, *The Peri Pascha Attributed to Melito of Sardis: Setting, Purpose, and Sources* (Providence, RI: Brown Judaic Studies, 2000), 115.

between human free choice and God's response (*P.P.*739–744). "There is no suggestion that sinfulness is itself communicated to Adam's progeny as in later Augustinian teaching."[17]

B. Christian Authors 180–250 CE

I.   *Irenaeus of Lyons*

Irenaeus of Lyons (*ca.*185) wrote primarily against Gnostic deterministic salvation in his famous work *Adversus Haereses*. "One position fundamental to Irenaeus is that man should come to moral good by the action of his own moral will, and not spontaneously and by nature."[18] Physical death for the human race from Adam's sin was not so much a punishment as God's gracious gift to prevent humans from living eternally in a perpetual state of struggling with sin (*Adv. haer.*3.35.2).

Irenaeus championed humanity's free will for four reasons: (1) to refute Gnostic Divine Unilateral Predetermination of Individuals' Eternal Destinies, (2) because humanity's persisting *imago Dei* (image of God within humans) demands a persisting free will, (3) scriptural commands demand free will for legitimacy, and (4) God's justice becomes impugned without free will (genuine, not Stoic "non-free free will"). These were non-negotiable "apostolic doctrines." Scholars Wingren and Donovan both identify Irenaeus' conception of the *imago Dei* as freedom of choice itself. As Donovan relates: "This strong affirmation of human liberty is at the same time a clear

---

[17] Hall (1978), xlii.

[18] John Lawson, *The Biblical Theology of Saint Irenaeus* (London: The Epworth Press, 1948), 203.

rejection of the Gnostic notion of predetermined natures."[19]

Andia clarified that God's justice requires free choice since Irenaeus believed God's providence created all persons equally.[20] In refuting Gnostic determinism (Divine Unilateral Predetermination of Individuals' Eternal Destinies), Irenaeus argues that God determines persons' eternal destinies through foreknowledge of the free choices of persons (*Adv. haer.*2.29.1; 4.37.2–5; 4.29.1–2; 3.12.2,5,11; 3.32.1; 4.14, 4.34.1, 4.61.2). Irenaeus attacked both Stoicism and Gnostic heresies because DUPIED made salvation by faith superfluous, and made Christ's incarnation unnecessary.[21] Irenaeus taught God's predestination. This was based on God's foreknowledge of human choices without God constraining the human will as in Gnostic determinism.[22]

Irenaeus denied that any event could ever occur outside of God's sovereignty (*Adv. haer.*2.5.4), but simultaneously emphasized residual human free choice to receive God's gift, which only then results in regeneration. "The essential principle in the concept of freedom appears first

---

[19] Gustaf Wingren, *Man and the Incarnation*, trans. by Ross Mackenzie (Lund: C.W.K. Gleerup, 1947; repr., London: Oliver and Boyd, 1959), 36; Mary Ann Donovan, "Alive to the Glory of God: A Key Insight in St. Irenaeus," *TS* 49 (1988): 291 citing *Adv. haer.*4.37.

[20] Ysabel de Andia, *Homo vivens: incorruptibilité et divinisation de l'homme selon Irénée de Lyons* (Paris: Études Augustiniennes, 1986), 131.

[21] E.P. Meijering, "Irenaeus' relation to philosophy in the light of his concept of free will," in E.P. Meijering, ed. *God Being History: Studies in Patristic Philosophy* (Amsterdam: North Holland Publishing, 1975), 23.

[22] James Beaven, *An Account of the Life and Times of S. Irenaeus* (London: Gilbert and Rivington, 1841), 165–166; F. Montgomery Hitchcock, *Irenaeus of Lugdunum: A Study of His Teaching* (Cambridge: Cambridge University Press, 1914), 260; Wingren (1947; repr., 1959), 35–36.

in Christ's status as the sovereign Lord, because for Irenaeus man's freedom is, strangely enough, a direct expression of God's omnipotence, so direct in fact, that a diminution of man's freedom automatically involves a corresponding diminution of God's omnipotence."[23] Although he exalted God's sovereignty, it was not (erroneously) defined as God receiving everything he desires.[24] The scholar Denis Minns correctly states, "Irenaeus would insist as vigorously as Augustine that nothing could be achieved without grace. But he would have been appalled at the thought that God would offer grace to some and withhold it from others."[25]

II. Clement of Alexandria and Tertullian

Clement of Alexandria (*ca.*190) strongly defends a residual human free choice after Adam (*Strom.*1.1; cf. 4.24, 5.14). Divine foreknowledge determines divine election (*Strom.*1.18; 6.14). Clement understood that God calls *all* (πάντων τοίνυν ἀνθρώπων)—every human, not a few of every kind of human—whereas, "the called" are those who respond. He believed that if God exercised Divine Unilateral Predetermination of Individuals' Eternal Destinies (as the Marcionites and Gnostics believed), then he would not be the just and good Christian God but the heretical God of Marcion (*Strom.*5.1).

Clement refuted the followers of the Gnostic Marcion who believed initial faith was God's gift. Why?—it robbed humans of free choice (*Strom.*2.3–4; cf. *Strom.*4.11, *Quis dives Salvetur* 10). Yet Clement does not believe free choice saves persons as a human work (cf. John 1:13). He teaches God must

---

[23] Wingren (1947; repr., 1959), 35–36.

[24] Explained later when discussing Augustine's later specific sovereignty view.

[25] Denis Minns, *Irenaeus* (Washington, DC: Georgetown University Press, 1994), 136.

first draw and call every human to himself, since all have the greatest need for the power of divine grace (*Strom.*5.1). God does not initiate a mystical (i.e., Neoplatonic) inward draw to each of his elect. Instead, the Father previously revealed himself and drew every human through Old Testament scripture, but now reveals himself and draws all humanity equally to himself through Christ and the New Testament (cf. John 12:32; *Strom.*7.1–2).[26]

Tertullian (*ca.*205) wrote that despite a corrupted nature, humans possess a residual capacity to accept God's gift based upon the good divine image (the "proper nature") still resident within every human (*De anima* 22). Every person retains the capacity to believe. He refuted Gnosticism's discriminatory deterministic salvation (*Val.*29). God remains sovereign while he permits good and evil, because he foreknows what will occur by human free choice (*Cult. fem.*2.10). Humans can and should respond to God by using their God-given innate *imago Dei* free choice. Therefore, Tertullian did not approve of an "innocent" infant being baptized before responding personally to God's gift of grace through hearing and believing the gospel (*De baptismo* 18). He believed that children should await baptism until they are old enough to personally believe in Christ.

III. Origen of Alexandria

Origen (*ca.*185–254) advances scriptural arguments for free choice that fill the third book of *De principiis* (*P. Arch.*3.1.6). "This also is definite in the teaching of the Church, every rational soul is possessed of free-will and volition" that can choose the good (*Princ.*, Pref.5). God does not coerce humans or directly influence individuals but instead only invites. Why?—

---

[26] Modern commentaries on this gospel rarely connect God's drawing as being through scripture and Christ (John 6:44–45; 5.38–47; 8.19, 31, 47; 12.32). Cf. 1 Pet. 2.2.

because God desires willing lovers. Just as Paul asked Philemon to voluntarily (κατὰ ἑκούσιον) act in goodness (Phlm. 1.14), so God desires uncoerced lovers (*Hom. Jer*.20.2). Origen explains how God hardens Pharaoh's heart. God sends divine signs/events that Pharaoh rejects and hardens his own heart. God's hardening is indirect. "Now these passages are sufficient of themselves to trouble the multitude, as if man were not possessed of free will, but as if it were God who saves and destroys whom he will" (*Princ.* 3.1.7). Origen distinguishes between God's temporal blessings and eternal destinies in Romans 9–11, rejecting the Gnostic eternal salvation view from these chapters.

Initial faith is human faith, not a divine gift. "The apostles, once under-standing that faith which is only human cannot be perfected unless that which comes from God should be added to it, they say to the Savior, 'Increase our faith.'" (*Com.Rom*.4.5.3). God desires to give the inheritance of the promises not as something due from debt but through grace. Origen says that the inheritance from God is granted to those who believe, not as the debt of a wage but as a gift of [human] faith (*Com.Rom*.4.5.1).[27]

Election is based upon divine foreknowledge. "For the Creator makes ves-sels of honor and vessels of dishonor, not from the beginning according to His foreknowledge, since He does not pre-condemn or pre-justify according to it; but (He makes) those into vessels of honor who purged themselves, and those into vessels of dishonor who allowed themselves to remain unpurged" (*P.Arch*.3.1.21). Origen does not refute divine foreknowledge resulting in election but refutes the philosophical view of foreknowledge as necessarily causative, which Celsus taught:

---

[27] This serves as an excellent example of a passage removed from its context by which some persons erroneously attempt to prove an early church father taught faith was God's gift.

Celsus imagines that an event, predicted through foreknowledge, comes to pass because it was predicted; but we do not grant this, maintaining that he who foretold it was not the cause of its happening, because he foretold it would happen; but the future event itself, which would have taken place though not predicted, afforded the occasion to him, who was endowed with fore-knowledge, of foretelling its occurrence (*C.Cels.*2.20).

Origen explains the Christian interpretation of Rom 9:16.[28] The Gnostic and heretical deterministic interpretations render God's words superfluous, and invalidate Paul's chastisements and approbations to Christians. Nevertheless, the human desire/will is *insufficient* to accomplish salvation, so Christians must rely upon God's grace (*P. Arch.*3.1.18). Origen does not minimize the innate human sin principle that incites persons to sin. Rather, he chastises immature Christians who blame their sins on the devil instead of their own passions (*Princ.*3.2.1–2; *P. Arch.*3.1.15).

IV. Cyprian and Novatian

Cyprian (d.254 CE) taught God stands sovereign (*Treat.*3.19; 5.56.8; 12.80). Yet, God rewards or punishes based upon his foreknowledge of human choices and responses (*Treat.*7.17, 19; *Ep.*59.2). Humans retain free choice despite Adam's sin (*Treat.*7.17, 19).[29] "That the liberty of believing or of not believing is placed in freedom of choice" (*Treat.*12.52). Jesus utilized persuasion, not force (*Treat.*9.6). Obedience resulting in martyrdom should arise from free choice, not necessity (*Treat.* 7.18), especially since imitating Christ restores God's likeness.

Novatian (*ca.*250 CE) teaches a personal responsibility for sin instead of guilt from Adam, because a person who is pre-determined due to (even fallen) nature cannot be held liable. Only a willful decision can incur guilt

---

[28] Rom. 9:16, "So it depends not upon man's will or exertion, but upon God's mercy."

[29] For a refutation of Cyprian as teaching Augustine's inherited guilt unto damnation see Wilson, *Augustine's Conversion*, 77–82.

(De cib. Jud.3). Lactantius *(ca.*315 CE) taught Adam's fall produced only physical death (not eternal death) through the loss of God's perpetually gifted immortality *(Inst.*2.13), as Williams correctly identified.[30] Yet, mortality in a corrupted human body predisposed the human race to sin *(Inst.*6.13). God loves every person equally, offers immortality equally to each person, and every human is capable of responding to God's offer—without divine intervention *(Div.inst.*5.15) "God, who is the guide of that way, denies immortality to no human being" but offers salvation equally to every person *(Div.inst.*6.3). Humanity must contend with its propensity to sin, but the corrupted nature provides no excuse since free choice persists *(Inst.*2.15; 4.24; 4.25; 5.1). He consistently teaches Christian free choice *(Inst.*5.10, 13, 14).

C. Christian Authors 250–400 CE

I. *Hilary of Poitiers*

Hilary (d.368 CE) referred to John 1:12–13 as God's offer of salvation that is equally offered to everyone. "They who do receive Him by virtue of their faith advance to be sons of God, being born not of the embrace of the flesh nor of the conception of the blood nor of bodily desire, but of God [...] the Divine gift is offered to all, it is no heredity inevitably imprinted but a prize awarded to willing choice" *(Trin.*1.10–11). Human nature has a propensity to evil *(Trin.*3.21; *Hom. Psa.*1.4) that is located in the physical body *(Hom. Psa.*1.13). Human free choice elicits the divine gift, yet the divine birth (through faith) belongs solely to God. A human 'will' cannot create the birth *(Trin.*12.56) yet that birth occurs through human faith.

---

[30] Norman Williams, *The Ideas of the Fall and Original Sin* from the Bampton Lectures, Oxford University, 1924 (London: Longmans, Green and Co., 1927), 297.

II. The Cappadocians

Gregory of Nazianzus (*ca*.329–389 CE) writes frequently of the "fall of sin" from Adam (*Or*.1; 33.9; 40.7), including the evil consequence of that original sin (*Or*.45.12). "We were detained in bondage by the Evil One, sold under sin, and receiving pleasure in exchange for wickedness" (*Or*.45.22). Salvation (not faith) is God's gift. "We call it the Gift, because it is given to us in return for nothing on our part" (*Or*.40.4). "This, indeed, was the will of Supreme Goodness, to make the good even our own, not only because it was sown in our nature, but because cultivated by our own choice, and by the motions of our free will to act in either direction." (*Or*.2.17). "Our soul is self-determining and independent, choosing as it will with sovereignty over itself that which is pleasing to it" (*Ref.Conf. Eun*.139). Children are born blameless (*Ep*.206). God is sovereign, and Christ died for all humankind, including the 'non-elect.' (*Or*.45.26; cf. *Or*.38.14). Nevertheless, in matters of personal salvation, God limits himself, allowing humans free choice (*Or*.32.25, 45.8).

Basil of Caesarea (*ca*.330–379 CE) believed humans do not inherit sin or evil, but choose to sin resulting in death. We control our own actions, proved by God's payment and punishment (*Hom. Hex*.2.4). He promotes God's sovereignty over human *temporal* (not eternal) destinies, including our time of death by "God who ordains our lots" (*Ep*.269) yet he refutes micromanaging Stoic Providence (*Ep*.151). God empowers human faith for great works because mere human effort cannot accomplish divine good (*Ep*.260.9). Basil allowed no place for either Chaldean astrological fatalism (*Hom. Hex*.6.5; *Ep*.236), or Divine Unilateral Predetermination of Individuals' Eternal Destinies. Righteous judgment resulting in reward and punishment demands Christian traditional free choice. In contrast, any concept of inevitable evil in humans necessarily destroys Christian hope (*Hom. Hex*.6.7) because all humans have an innate natural reason with the ability to do good and avoid evil (*Hom. Hex.*8.5; cf. *Ep.*260.7). Basil refuted a dozen heresies, but reserved his strongest denunciation for the one teaching determinism—"the detestable Manichaean heresy" (*Hom. Hex.*2.4).

Gregory Nyssen (*ca.*335–395 CE) pervasively teaches a post-Adamic congenital weakness, inclined to evil and in slavery to sin but *without* guilt (*C. Eun.*1.1; 3.2–3; 3.8; *De opificio hom.*193; *Cat. mag.*6, 35; *Ep.*18; *Ref. conf. Eun.*; *Dial. anim. et res.*, etc.). Each person's alienation from God occurs through personal sin and vice, not Adam's sin (*C. Eun.*3.10). Despite an inherited tendency to evil, the divine image within humans retains goodness, just as Tertullian and others had taught (*Opif. hom.*164; cf. *Ep.*3.17).[31] Humanity's ruin and inability to achieve eternal life by self-effort demanded God initiate the rescue through Christ (*Ref. conf. Eun.*418–20). But Gregory refutes the idea of a human nature so corrupted that it would render an individual incapable of a genuine choice to receive God's readily available gift of grace offered to everyone equally.

By appealing to the justice of God's recompenses, Gregory refutes those [e.g., Manichaeans] who believe humans are born sinful and thus culpable (*De anim.*120). The choice for salvation belongs to humans, apart from God's manipulation, coercion, or unilateral intervention (*C. Eun.*3.1.116–18; cf. *Adv. Mac. spir. sancto* 105–6; *De virginitate* 12.2–3). Gregory upholds Christian [not Stoic] divine sovereignty (*Ref. conf. Eun.* 169; cf. 126–27; *Opif. hom.*185).

III. Methodius, Theodore, and Ambrose

Methodius (d.312 CE) believed all humans retain genuine free will even after Adam's fall since Christian free choice was necessary for God to be just in rewarding the good and punishing the wicked (*Symp.*8.16; *PG* 18:168d). He

---

[31] *C. Eunomium* 24 (on the soul's ability to see Christ) is probably post-baptismal.

championed traditional Christian free choice in a major work against Gnostic determinism (*Peri tou autexousiou,* 73–77).[32] Cyril of Jerusalem (*ca.*348–386 CE) taught humans enter this world sinless (*Cat.*4.19) and God's foreknowledge of human responses determines the divine choosing of them for service (*Cat.*1.3).

Theodore of Mopsuestia (*ca.*350–428 CE) defended traditional original sin against Manichaean damnable inherited guilt (*Adv. def. orig. pecc.*), so that, "Man's freedom takes the first step, which is afterwards made effective by God . . . [with] the will of each man as being absolutely free and unbiased and able to choose either good or evil."[33] Humans retain the ability to choose good and evil (*Comm. Ioh.*5.19).

Ambrose of Milan (d.397 CE) baptized Augustine in Milan on Easter in 387 CE. He taught traditional (not Augustinian) original sin (*De fide* 5.5, 8, 60; *Exc. Satyri* 2.6; cf. 1.4). Ambrose believed slavery to sin [the sin propensity] was inherited, but this was not literal sin that produced personal culpability and damnation (*De Abrah.*2.79). The scholar Paul Blowers noted, "Ambrosiaster (Rom.5:12ff) and Ambrose (*Enar.in Ps.*38.29) ... both

---

[32] *Patrologia orientalis* 22:797–801. Cf. Roberta Franchi, *Metodio di Olimpo: Il libero arbitrio* (Milano: Paoline, 2015).

[33] Henry Wace, *A Dictionary of Christian Biography and Literature to the End of the Sixth Century A.D., with an Account of the Principal Sects and Heresies* (London: Murray, 1911), "Theodore, III.B.f." This suggests Macarius was incorrect when he assumed that this work by Theodore was anti-Augustinian. It is defending traditional freedom of choice versus eternal damnation by inherited sin from being born physically, a Manichaean doctrine. The quotation is from Reginald Moxon, *The Doctrine of Sin* (London: George Allen and Unwin, 1922), 40.

authors concluded that individuals were ultimately accountable only for their own sins."[34]

Ambrose emphasized God predestined individuals based upon his fore-knowledge of the future, concerning which God was omniscient (*Ep.*57; *De fide* 2.11, 97). God compels no one, but patiently waits for a human response in order that He may provide grace, preferring pity over punishment (*Paen.*1.5). He insisted upon residual free choice and views an increase in a person's faith (not initial faith) as a divine gift given in response to faithfulness. (*Paen.*1.48; *Ep.*41.6).

D. Conclusion

Not even one early church father writing from 95–430 CE—despite abundant acknowledgement of inherited human depravity—considered Adam's fall to have erased human free choice to independently respond to God's gracious invitation.[35] God did not give initial faith as a gift. Humans could do nothing to save themselves—only God's grace could save. Total inability to do God's good works without God's grace did not mean inability to believe in Christ and prepare for baptism. No Christian author embraced deterministic Divine Unilateral Predetermination of Individuals' Eternal Destinies (DUPIED): all who considered it rejected DUPIED as an erroneous pagan Stoic or Neoplatonic philosophy, or a Gnostic or Manichaean heresy, unbefitting Christianity's gracious relational God. God's gift was salvation by divine grace through human faith (cf. Eph. 2:8), not a unilateral initial faith gift, as the

---

[34] Paul Blowers, "Original Sin," in Everett Ferguson, ed. *Encyclopedia of Early Christianity*. 2nd edn. (New York, NY: Routledge, 1999), 839–840.

[35] See Wilson, *Augustine's Conversion*, Appendix III (pp. 307–9) for a complete list of early church authors on this topic.

Gnostics and Manichaean heretics were claiming. Early Christian literature could be distinguished from Gnostic and Manichaean literature by this essential element.

In a seemingly rare theological unanimity over hundreds of years and throughout the entire Mediterranean world, a Christian *regula fidei* (rule of faith) of free choice (advocated by Origen as *the* rule of faith) combated the Divine Unilateral Predetermination of Individuals' Eternal Destinies espoused in Stoicism's "non-free free will" and Gnosticism's divine gift of infused initial faith into a "dead will." The loving Christian God allowed humans to exercise their God-given free will.

Chapter 3
Augustine of Hippo's Traditional Theology 386–411 CE

Augustine was baptized into Christianity in 386 CE by his spiritual father, Ambrose, bishop of Milan. The early Augustine gradually moved away from Neoplatonic and Manichaean ideas to embrace the Christian theology of his time. A decade later Augustine discovered God's grace apart from the merit of human works after reading the commentaries of Victorinus and then Jerome on Galatians.[1] When he became co-bishop of Hippo, Augustine was teaching traditional theology against the Manichaean heretics, as Christian leaders had taught for centuries against the Stoics and Gnostics. God's responses to humans and God's election to heavenly bliss were based upon God's foreknowledge of future human choices, not a unilateral and non-relational pre-determinism (as in Augustine's prior Gnostic Manichaeism, Stoicism, and Neoplatonism).[2] Augustine taught this traditional Christian

---

[1] Stephen Cooper, *Marius Victorinus' Commentary on Galatians: Introduction, Translation, and Notes* (Oxford: Oxford University Press, 2005), 136–139; Andrew Cain, *St. Jerome: Commentary on Galatians* in The Fathers of the Church (Washington, DC: The Catholic University of America Press, 2010), 16–33.

[2] Because God is omnitemporal, the term "foreknowledge" is an anthropomorphism. God lives in the past, present, and future simultaneously. See Richard Swinburne, "God and Time," in Eleonore Stump, ed., *Reasoned Faith* (Ithaca: Cornell University Press, 1993), 204–222.

theology, defending human free choice and election based upon God's foreknowledge for over twenty-five years until 412 CE.[3]

A. Augustine's Works 386–395 CE

The early Augustine's traditional theology pervasively asserts that humans can respond to God without divine assistance. "But miserable friends could be masters of this world if they were willing to be the sons of God, for God has given them the power to become his sons" (*Ver. rel.*65). Contrary to the Manichaean misinterpretation of Ephesians 2:3 ("were by nature children of wrath" meaning at birth), Augustine denounced alienation from God by nature, "Remember what the apostle said, 'In our lifestyle [behavior] we are alienated from God,'" and, "Augustine said: 'I say it is not sin, if it be not sinned by one's own will; hence also there is [a] reward, because of our own will we do right'" (*c.Fort.*21). Augustine clarifies that his free will statements concern current persons, not merely Adam's original nature.

> For this reason, those souls, whatever they do, if by nature and not voluntarily, that is, if they lack the movement of the free soul/mind of doing and not doing, if, in short, no power is granted to them to abstain from their own deeds, we are not able to lay hands on their sin. But all admit, both bad souls are justly condemned and those who have not sinned are unjustly condemned. (*an.im-mor.*17; cf.,12; translation mine).

"For by his free will man has a means to believe in the Liberator and to receive grace" (*exp.prop.Rm.*44.3). God's foreknowledge allows him to predestine only those whom he knows will respond in faith: "Nor did God predestine anyone except him whom he knew would believe and would

---

[3] Virtually all scholars claim Augustine converted to his novel theology in 396/7 CE with *Ad Simplicianum* 1.2. I have demonstrated that Augustine revised this work just as he revised others many decades after they were written. See Wilson, *Augustine's Conversion*, 134–156 and Wilson, "Re-dating Augustine's *Ad Simplicianum* 1.2 to the Pelagian Controversy," *St.Patr.* XCVIII, vol.24 (2017): 431–450.

follow the call, whom he [Paul] calls 'the elect.' (5) For many do not come, though they have been called." (*exp.prop.Rm.*55).

"By all means he has mercy on whom he wants, and he hardens whom he wants, but this will of God cannot be unjust. For it springs from deeply hidden merits [*occultissimis meritis*] because, even though sinners themselves have constituted a single mass on account of the sin of all, still it is not the case that there is no difference among them" (*Div.Q.O.*68.4; *cf.,* 82.2). "Through foreknowledge God chooses believers and damns unbelievers" (*exp.prop.Rm.*62.15). "Therefore God did not elect anyone's works [which God himself will grant] by foreknowledge, but rather by foreknowledge he chose faith, so that he chooses precisely him whom he foreknew would believe in him; and to him he gives the Holy Spirit. ... Belief is our work, but good deeds are his who gives the Holy Spirit to believers" (*exp.prop.Rm.*60.11–12). In agreement with all other extant early Christian writings, Augustine viewed free will as critical to defending the Christian God against the highly deterministic Gnostic and Manichaean heresies and from Stoic fate.

> Now however, when God punishes a sinner what else do you suppose he will say to him than "Why did you not use your freewill for the purpose for which I gave it to you, that is, in order to do right?"... For neither is it sin nor done right, because it [choice] is not made voluntarily. For this reason both punishment and reward would be unjust, if man did not have free will. (*lib.arb.*2.3, translation mine)

"Scripture teaches that God himself placed this in our power when it says, 'He gave them the power to become sons of God' [John 1:12]. But people are called sons of the devil when they imitate his impious pride, fall away from the light and the height of wisdom, and do not believe the truth" (*c.Adim.*5).

B. Augustine's Works 396–411 CE

Scholars identify *Ad Simplicianum* of 396 CE as Augustine's transition to his later theology, incited by reading Romans, Galatians, and 1 Corinthians.[4] This one letter to bishop Simplicianus of Milan, Italy from North Africa demonstrates a sudden shift in theology from the first half to the second half of the same letter. The first half teaches Augustine's and Christianity's traditional free choice, but the second half abruptly changes (in section five) to doctrines not associated with any prior Christian author.

Explanations for this anomaly have been few and inadequate. Why? Because Augustine falls silent for another fifteen years about these new ideas. Prior to my research, no scholarly work researched Augustine's entire corpus chronologically from 386–430 CE specifically analyzing his five final doctrines of: 1.) God giving initial faith as a gift, 2.) inherited damnable *reatus* (guilt) from Adam, 3.) the gift of perseverance, 4.) divine unilateral predetermination of persons' eternal destinies independent of God's foreknowledge, and 5.) God's neither desiring nor providing for the salvation of all persons. By assuming a transition at 396 CE, scholars did not diligently research Augustine's works from 386 to 411 CE.

When these works are read chronologically, one finds Augustine teaching—for the next fifteen years—the exact same doctrines he has taught for the prior decades. He defends God's foreknowledge of human choices as

---

[4] James Wetzel, "Simplicianum, Ad," in Allan Fitzgerald, ed. *Augustine Through the Ages: An Encyclopedia* (Grand Rapids, MI: Eerdmans, 1999), 798–799; Peter Brown, *Augustine of Hippo: A Biography* (London: Faber and Faber, 1967; rev. edn. Berkeley, CA: University of California Press, 2000), 147–148; Ernest Evans, *Tertullian's Homily on Baptism* (London: SPCK, 1964), 101; Paul Rigby, "Original Sin," in Allan Fitzgerald, ed. *Augustine Through the Ages: An Encyclopedia* (Grand Rapids, MI: Eerdmans, 1999), 607–614; Carol Harrison, *Rethinking Augustine's Early Theology: An Argument for Continuity* (Oxford: Oxford University Press, 2006); etc., as listed in Wilson, *Augustine's Conversion.*

important in divine election, humans remain capable of choosing the good and God, humans are not damned at birth (as the Manichaeans taught), and God loves every individual and desires salvation for every human.

In 398 CE, Augustine states Felix may become a Christian by examining the evidence, without God regenerating the will or providing a gift of faith (*Fel*.2.12). When citing John 1:12–13, God does not give persons the power to believe: He is the power of those who do believe and trust him (*Fel*.1.12). Initial faith is not a gift from God since persons can still believe by their own power. Augustine accuses Felix and Manichaeism of abusing the phrase 'free will.' They render it meaningless since those who are 'not willing' were *not even capable* of willing good. He exposes the Manichaean's clever omission of overt 'compulsion' (*Fel*.2.5) when abusing the term 'free will.'

In 399 CE he writes against Faustus the Manichaean. When discussing Romans 9, Augustine says God's determinations are secret, he still judges justly by punishing those who refuse him; and, humanity retains a free will, not a will that can only sin (*Faust*.21.2–3). Furthermore, he accuses the Manichaean god of baiting the damned with an impossible dilemma. He again exposes the Manichaean ploy of justifying their unjust determinism through a mere semblance or facade of personal choice in free will. Augustine vehemently argues that the Manichaeans create a shockingly cruel and criminal God who condemns persons to eternal punishment by something necessarily intrinsic to them. Here the Manichaean god is shockingly unjust:

> And for this reason it remains for you to say that those souls destined to be condemned with eternal bonds in the horrible sphere emerged as enemies of the holy light not by their own will but by necessity, and it remains for you to make your god the sort of a judge before whom nothing could help those whose case you defend, once you have demonstrated the necessity of their action, and the sort of king from whom you are not able to obtain forgiveness for your brothers, his [own] sons and members whose enmities against you and against him you say emerged not by will but by necessity. O monstrous cruelty! (*Faust*.22.22)

In 401 CE, Augustine proves God's goodness with a long list of scriptures. Christianity's God in compassionate mercy and grace patiently desires all sinners to return in humility: God does not desire any of their deaths (*Nat. bon.*48). In *De bono conuigali* (401 CE), Augustine views only mortality as the punishment for Adam's sin (*Bon. conj.*2). The human soul possesses great strength for serving righteousness rather than lusts (*Bon. conj.*34).

When challenged by Petilianus (401 CE), Augustine had no solution to the tension of human free will and God's drawing of people to himself. Petilianus taught unilateral determinism. He used John 6:44 ("No one comes to me unless the Father draws him," RSV) to challenge Augustine's belief in human free choice in salvation. Augustine avoids answering Petilianus' question while emphasizing free will (*C. litt. Petil.*2.185–186).

About 403 CE, free choice did not end with Adam but persists, because God (in His foreknowledge) knew some persons would by their own choice desire to seek and serve Him willingly (*Catech. rud.*30). Christianity's relational God still responds to human attitudes and choices. Augustine cites Eph. 2:8–10 explaining gratuitous salvation and good works but *without* mentioning initial faith to believe in Christ as a divine gift (*Virginit.*41).

In his *Confessions* (*ca.*397–403 CE),[5] Augustine does not deviate from his traditional theology. Consistent with all of his other works from 397–405 CE, Augustine teaches original sin but *without* inherited damnable guilt. God acts in response to persons instead of unilaterally determining eternal destinies. Every person possesses residual free choice to believe God's revelation of salvation in Christ without requiring God's gift of initial faith. Anyone

---

[5] Books X–XIII were written in 403 CE according to Pierre-Marie Hombert, *Nouvelles recherches sur la chronologie Augustinienne* (Paris: Institut d'Études Augustiniennes, 2000).

finding theological alterations in *Confessions* must impose these by assuming a prior shift in Augustine's theology in 396 CE.[6]

About 404 CE, Augustine praised the faith of the thief on the cross as sufficient for salvation *without* water baptism (*Bapt.*4.29–30). Baptism only avails for infants' dedication to God and a first step toward salvation, not the forgiveness of guilt from original sin (*Bapt.*4.32). Augustine requires a conversion of the heart (4.33) and perseverance to the end for salvation (*Bapt.*1.14) without mentioning God giving these as gifts.

In 402–405 CE, the certainty of God's prophecies is not determined by unilateral foreordination, but (still) by God's foreknowledge of "future" human free choices (*Unit. eccl.*23 and 73). Augustine's traditional understanding of predestination (*predestinata*) continues with God's foreknowledge relationally responding to "future" human free choices, not his later DUPIED (*Unit. eccl.*23, 34, 39, 52).

About 409 CE, salvation was not withheld from anyone who was worthy of it. The only persons *not* worthy of salvation were ones God's foreknowledge identified as rebuffing his grace (*ep.*102.15). The penalty for Adam's sin was mortality (not eternal death), with immortality being recoverable through God's mercy (*Mus.*6.33). Despite Adam's fall, the fall of each person's soul into sin and damnation remains private, not corporate in Adam (*Mus.*6.53).

Therefore, from his conversion in 386 CE until 411 CE, Augustine taught traditional Christian doctrines against Gnostic-Manichaean divine unilateral determinism. None of his later doctrines now associated with Calvinism can

---

[6] For a response to Paul Rigby, *Original Sin in Augustine's* Confessions (Ottawa: University of Ottawa Press, 1987), esp. 42, see Wilson, *Augustine's Conversion*, 125–130.

be found for twenty-five years. There are two minor exceptions. Both are due to his later revisions of his own works.

C. Two Pre-412 Anomalies

Starting in 412 CE during his conflict with the Pelagians (as we will see in the next chapter),[7] Augustine changes his theology by teaching the loss of human free will, damnable guilt at birth, initial faith being a unilateral gift of God without human involvement, and God giving the gift of perseverance to only some Christians. But from 386–411 CE, only a portion (not the whole) of two works are at variance with his prior traditional Christian views. His *De libero arbitrio* 3.47–54 and *Ad Simplicianum* 2.5–22 contain sections contradicting his prior and subsequent traditional doctrines.

I.   Lib. arb.3.47–54 (On Free Will)

In *De libero arbitrio* 2.1–3.46 (395 CE) a serious anomaly appears. Despite Augustine's traditional theology persisting until 412 CE, a sudden and dramatic shift in tone and substance occurs in *Lib. arb.*3.47–54 allegedly written seventeen years earlier with the remainder of this work.[8] The following nine points are technical and may be reviewed in support of the argument.

There are nine reasons for considering *Lib. arb.*3.47–54 to be a later revision by Augustine over fifteen years later in early 412 CE:

1.) Evodius (who was absent for forty chapters) introduces this section, making a one paragraph cameo appearance requesting an explanation for differences in 'the wills' of individuals, then permanently

---

[7] See Chapter 4 for explanations of the Pelagian controversy.

[8] Roland Teske, *"Libero arbitrio, De,"* in Allan D. Fitzgerald, ed. *Augustine Through the Ages: An Encyclopedia*. Grand Rapids, MI: Eerdmans, 1999), 494–495; he noted the change but did not list nine reasons.

disappears.

2.) Augustine's prior philosophical complaisant tone suddenly converts to a pompous moralizing exegesis of the book of Genesis explaining the horrendous effects on all humanity from Adam's primal sin.

3.) Only fifteen biblical quotations occur in the entire third book; but suddenly, an unprecedented four scriptures are successively cited (3.51), and six occur within these few chapters, comprising forty percent of all scriptural citations within book 3. This matches his post-411 CE proof-text[9] citation cluster pattern.

4.) An outburst of twelve first-person plural verbs occurs in the three chapters 3.52–54. In contrast, *Lib. arb.*3.47–51 contain none, and the count in the final twenty-seven chapters (3.55–77) is only seventeen with a maximum of four in *Lib. arb.*3.60. The entire book (3.1–77) contains only forty appearances. Thus, less than four percent of book three contains thirty percent of these uses.[10]

5.) Augustine concludes 3.47–54 by quoting Eph. 2:3, "by nature we were children of wrath," its first proof-text appearance in any of his works, letters, or sermons, and surprisingly absent until 412 CE.

6.) The prior discussion of God's foreknowledge in relation to free will (*Lib. arb.*3.4–11) was concluded with "God has foreknowledge of all his own actions, but is not the agent of all he foreknows" (3.11). This

---

[9] A verse used as a theological hammer by pulling it out of its context and floating it in thin air.

[10] The closest contenders are 3.59–61 with twenty-four percent and 3.35–37 with fifteen percent, while 3.28 alone contains fifteen percent. This in itself cannot prove that this outburst in three chapters constitutes a proof for a later revision. However, it is the largest cluster in this book. Combined with the other eight reasons, this clustering is suggestive of a revision by Augustine.

conclusion follows Origen's rebuttal of pagan causal foreknowledge. But then this topic incongruously reappears immediately to introduce this amended section in 3.47.

7.) For the first time in all his works *peccatum* (sin) means "the necessary penalty of that first sin" (3.54) instead of "committed knowingly and with free will."

8.) For the first time the (Stoic) 'evil will' is the cause of all evils (3.48–49), freedom of the will is lost (3.52, 54), and humans are powerless to do good (3.51, 52, 53). Only a few paragraphs prior, humans required "free will and sufficient power" as prerequisites for being assigned guilt (*Lib. arb.*3.45). But suddenly humans now have no power for good as a punishment for Adam's sin (3.51). The powerful 'carnal custom' prevents persons from *choosing* good (3.52) as the heretofore minimal 'ignorance and difficulty' command center stage (3.52). Adam's willful sin receives the inherited just penalty of not only losing the power to *do* right (Romans 7) but to even *know* what is right (3.52).

9.) Finally, if 3.47–3.54 is omitted, the contextual argument of *Lib. arb.* 3.55 naturally follows 3.46. Augustine in 3.46 had argued for personal guilt only from personal sin through current free will and sufficient power to choose good, (note 'His creatures,' 'you,' and 'no person'), and 3.44 affirms "there is no guilt if they are what they are because they did not receive the power." As 3.46 confers, "Sin arises only when a man departs from his truth." Correspondingly, in 3.55 (immediately after the revision), Augustine discusses our mortal births into ignorance and difficulty from Adam and Eve. But their offspring can will to turn to God who provides power to transcend that inherited ignorance and difficulty. *Lib. arb.*3.55 follows perfectly after 3.46 as if originally written to follow it. His theology both immediately before and after contradicts the revised section 3.47–54.

These nine facts stand in direct opposition to the remainder of this entire treatise. Combined with his abrupt transition in a small section (3.47–54), this proves difficult to explain. Indeed, *Lib. arb.*3.47–54 sticks out like a sore thumb, a previously unparalleled anomalous section. Something reversed Augustine's mind within a few sentences in the middle of this work, contradicting everything prior and following. Incredibly, this novel theology cannot be found in his subsequent works until 412 CE. Most importantly, his subsequent chapters (3.55 to the end) reiterate the prior traditional themes of *Lib. arb.*1.1–3.46. In these sections, humans possess freedom of 'will' (3.55, 74), an innate God-given capacity for good and seeking God that procures God's aid (3.56, 58, 60, 65). The soul possesses the power to seek diligently and piously with God's help for righteousness, and natural ignorance and impotence are *not* culpable since only failure to seek knowledge results in guilt (3.60, 64); and, Augustine wants to avoid saying, "we sinned in Adam" (3.56).

The scholar Teske also noted Augustine's abrupt alterations in tone and content.[11] We must consider that this radical shift represents a later revision by Augustine. To anyone pursuing a meticulous chronological reading of Augustine's works, *Lib. arb.*3.47–54 represents an inexplicable, *unacknowledged* anomaly. Yet the scholar DeBuhn attributes the debate with Fortunatus (*ca.*392) as inspiring Augustine's third and final view of grace with "a greatly vitiated will, retaining only the fig-leaf of an original free will in Adam (*Lib. arb* 3.18.51–3.20.55)" about 395 CE. He does not recognize this

---

[11] Teske (1999), 494–495.

as Augustine's 412 CE revision of it.[12] Nevertheless, the inherited damnable *reatus* (guilt from Adam), found in his later works, remains absent. Here, infant baptism is not yet required for salvation from damnation due to "Augustinian" original sin (*Lib. arb.*3.66), despite infant baptism for salvation being the very foundation of his later theology.

But if this is Augustine's revised addition, why does no existing manuscript have 3.47–54 absent as in the original? Because, even if the original work in 396 (cf., *ep.*31) excluded 3.47–54, Augustine's own revised library copy would take preferential authority for his librarian (Possidius) and the ancient world. Augustine's personal copies from his library would be considered more reliable and would therefore replace other copies considered defective and missing his revisions. Others had not been copied from Augustine's own library and were inferior. Augustine personally revised many texts but we do not possess even one with variants, even with works where Augustine acknowledges *explicit* revisions up to twenty years after the original work (as discussed in the next chapter). Therefore, no manuscript copy with a variant lacking 3.47–54 should be expected.

The problem of the very premature theology of *Lib. arb.*3.47–54 (395 CE) screams for an explanation with no evidence for any theological change in any other work for another seventeen years. It is the only section that deviates from traditional theology, and surprisingly, following which Augustine immediately reverts to his traditional theology in *Lib. arb.*3.55 as if the interposed 3.47–54 had never been written. Augustine revised numerous works

---

[12] Jason BeDuhn, "Did Augustine Win His Debate with Fortunatus?" in Jacob van den Berg, Annemaré Kotzé, Tobias Nicklas, and Madeleine Scopello, eds. *'In Search of Truth': Augustine, Manichaeism and other Gnosticism–Studies for Johannes van Oort at Sixty*, NHMS 74 (Leiden: Brill, 2011), 475; he suggests Fortunatus won the debate.

many years or decades later. The most critical ones that he revised are *De libero arbitrio* 3.47–54 and *Ad Simplicianum* 2.5–22. We are now prepared to examine *Ad Simplicianum.*

II. The Letter to Bishop Simplicianus 396/7 CE

Authored in 396/7 CE, the second half of *Ad Simplicianum* contains numerous extremely detailed and new dogmatic theologies that cannot be found for another fifteen years in any of his subsequent twenty-seven works from 396–411 CE. The scholar Wetzel emphasizes, "In striking contrast to the rest of the work, the second part of book 1, on Romans 9:19–20, sets off a veritable revolution in his theology."[13] Indeed, *Ad Simplicianum* erupts like the explosive volcano Krakatoa with a dozen novel theological concepts and terms that do not appear again for fifteen years.[14]

The scholar Babcock asserts, "In particular, he excludes the idea that God chose Jacob because he foreknew Jacob's faith. The thin line of demarcation between foreknowledge of faith and foreknowledge of works had proved too fine, too fragile, for Augustine to wish to maintain it any longer."[15] Babcock accurately describes Augustine combining faith as a type of work. But note carefully (contrary to Babcock's assertion) that Augustine does *not* state, "God's election is *not* based upon foreknowledge." Rather, Augustine correctly stresses that Paul's *argumentative point* was not "election is based upon foreknowledge." Instead, Paul's emphasis was 'Jacob's election was *not* based upon *works*.' Perhaps the three-hundred-year-old traditional theology prohibited Augustine's overt denial of election based on divine

---

[13] Wetzel (1999), 798–799.

[14] Wilson, *Augustine's Conversion*, 139–155, which includes a discussion of other works Augustine revised.

[15] Babcock (1979): 55–74.

foreknowledge.

As will be demonstrated, Augustine's revised terms and his new interpretation of Romans 11 in *Ad Simplicianum* cannot be found in his writings for the next fifteen years. This occurs despite his multiple references to punishment for Adam's sin, infant baptism, the sin nature, and numerous citations of Romans 11 (none of which match this interpretation). Moreover, the few other previous times the term *massa* (lump) of humanity appears (e.g., *Div. quaest.* 68; *Conf.*13.15; *Faust.*22.22), all lack the theory of inherited guilt (*reatus*) since Christ came from that same *massa* (*Fel.*2.11). He then allegorizes an irrelevant passage from *Sir.* 21 trying to justify God: there is no unrighteousness with God despite God's unjust punishments. Augustine obviously feels a need to defend his novel interpretation (*Simpl.*2.20). His context in the next chapter does not concern initial faith but Christian progressive faith that allows growth in godliness. Indeed, *Ad Simplicianum* erupts with a dozen novel theological concepts:

1.)   *Massa peccati (mass of sin)*: *Massa* occurs four times   (*Simpl.*2.16, 17, 19, 20). This is as many times here within five brief chapters of *Simpl.*2 as in all of his other prior works combined.

2.)   *Traduce peccati (inherited sin)*: This term does not occur again for another fifteen years but is conveniently slipped in alongside the traditional doctrine of inherited mortality.

3.)   *Originali reatu (original guilt)*: This term also cannot be found for another fifteen years. Prior to 412 CE, Augustine does use a related term *originale peccatum* (original sin, not original guilt) four times (*Gen. Man.*2.10, *Ver. rel.*1.13, *Div. quaest.*88, *Conf.*5.9) but all carry the traditional prior meaning. Even in the first half of the book (*Simpl.*1), we find three references to traditional original sin, with none in *Simpl.*2, where *originali reatu* replaces it. However, after 412 CE, we find fifty-three occurrences. Thirty-seven of these are found in the anti-Pelagian writings.

He gave eight sermons with nine references (*S*.25, 56.9, 69.3, 136.9, 136.9, 143.1, 351.2, 362.14, 391). Then in June 413 CE in *S*.294, five references erupt in one sermon (a clustering pattern). Two epistles (*ep*.215; *ep*.157) contain two each. His prior traditional Christian understanding of original sin was an inherited *ignorance* and *difficulty* with the sin propensity (from *concupiscentia carnis/carnalis*, cf. *Lib. arb*.3.19, *Exp. Gal*.46, *Exp.quaest. Rom*. 1.13). This suddenly transforms into his later Augustinian original guilt. "But carnal concupiscence [the sin nature] now reigns as the result of the punishment for [Adam's] sin, having lumped the entire human race into one mass of permanent confusion and original guilt."[16] This novel meaning then completely disappears until fifteen years later where it is found in *Pecc. merit*.2.15.[17]

4.) Faith becomes "meritorious" and lumped with works, opposing Rom. 4:4–6 which distinguishes faith as NOT meritorious in the same sense works might be. This contradicts his own works after 395 CE (upon learning about unmerited grace from Victorinus and Jerome). This also contradicts his subsequent twenty-seven works until 412 CE.

5.) God's foreknowledge in election suffers an unexplained rejection despite the 1 Pet. 1:1–2 passage ("elect . . . according to the foreknowledge of God") and his centuries-old self-imposed universal Christian *rule of faith* on this very doctrine.

6.) God "justly" makes persons "vessels of perdition" in order to warn the righteous as to what will happen to them if they fall into unrighteousness.

7.) Free will exists but can only produce evil because humans are now sold under the totally corrupted sin nature (Stoic "non-free free will").

---

[16] Translation mine.

[17] Cf. Keech (2010), 113.

Human "wills" are Stoic/Neoplatonic/Manichaean "evil wills" by (fallen) nature.

8.)   Faith must be a gift like everything else. This is "proven" by appeal to 1 Cor. 4:7 despite this verse being used extensively in his other works until 412 CE without this novel interpretation of the verse. (This interpretation follows his Christian Donatist predecessor Tichonius from whom he borrowed much theology.)

9.)   Humans who previously hardened their own hearts becomes transformed into God's unwillingness to be merciful. This contrasts with subsequent works for the next fifteen years which argue for a just punishment for obstinate sinners because they refuse to believe when all persons are capable of exercising faith.

10.) God's efficacious calling (it cannot be resisted and it will succeed) replaces his prior Christian universal calling to which everyone can respond (but many do not). The universal calling (which equally calls all persons) still appears in his works, sermons, and letters from 396–412 CE.

11.) 'The will' commands center stage such that persons are not elected but amazingly only "wills" are elected—contradicting his prior argument in *Exp. quaest. Rom.* 37.3.

12.) God's justice must be defended by a hidden equity in an arbitrary election to provide grace and faith for righteous living (*Simpl.*2.16, 17, 18, 22). His explanations of Romans 11 for the next fifteen years fail to present his new defense.

Furthermore, Augustine contradicts his own theology within the alleged same letter to Simplicianus. The reply to Romans 7 (in question one) precisely reproduces his prior theology of non-Augustinian original sin (weakening but not rendering free will dead/inoperative). The one thing persons still retain in free will is the power to turn to God for help (*Simpl.*1.14). The human addiction to sinful pleasure does not arise from original sin but from the habit of repetitive sinning (1.10). The grace of God sets us free if we in faith yield ourselves to God (*Simpl*.1.11).

In contrast, his responses to the "second question" (*Ad Simplicianum* 2.5) totally reverse not only every prior extant Christian author, but also Augustine's very same letter (*Simpl*.1), all of Augustine's prior works, and his works for the next fifteen years. Something is seriously amiss.

D. Conclusion

The logical conclusion is that Augustine's invention of his new theology did not occur in 396 CE as scholars have taught but in 412 CE as he fought the Pelagians. If the small sections of *Simpl*.2.5–22 and *Lib. arb*.3.47–54 are temporarily excised from his massive number of works, absolutely *nothing* remains to prove Augustine transitioned to his later theology in 396/7 CE. These two contradictory anomalous sections within the same larger work (*Simpl*.2.5–22 and *Lib. arb*.3.47–54) match numerous other works which Augustine himself revised. That is, Augustine did not give any indication he had later personally revised these works. He places his newer theology right alongside the old without changing his prior writings. Furthermore, within the one year of 412 CE Augustine struggles to birth his new theology. This birthing process appears chronologically in his works, sermons, and letters all simultaneously.[18] We can now explore how and why Augustine births his new theology in the next chapter.

---

[18] Wilson, *Augustine's Conversion*, 215–240.

Chapter 4
Augustine's Conversion to "Non-free Free Will"

When Rome fell to the Vandals in 410 CE, Pelagius and Caelestius came to Augustine's home of North Africa (present day Tunisia) instigating the infamous Pelagian controversy.[1] These Pelagian Christians were reportedly teaching doctrines not accepted by other churches. For example, Adam's fall was merely a personal moral failure so each human born remained in the same state as Adam when Adam was created. There was no traditional Christian original sin (a sin propensity, moral weakness, and mandatory physical death).[2] But the Pelagians had no answer as to why infants were being baptized.[3] Jerome, Augustine, and numerous other Christian leaders

---

[1] N. Joseph Torchia, Creatio Ex Nihilo and the Theology of St. Augustine: The Anti-Manichaean Polemic and Beyond (New York: Peter Lang, 1999), 239.

[2] David Weaver, "From Paul to Augustine: Romans 5:12 in Early Christian Exegesis," St. Vladimir's Theological Quarterly 27.3 (1983), 187-206 and "The Exegesis of Romans 5:12 Among the Greek Fathers and Implications for the Doctrine of Original Sin: The 5th-12th Centuries," 29.2 (1985), 154-6; Johannes van Oort, "Augustine on Sexual Concupiscence and Original Sin," St.Patr.22 (Louvain: Peeters, 1989), 261. But see Alice Bonner, The Myth of Pelagianism British Academy Monographs (Oxford: Oxford University Press, 2018) who argues Pelagius did not deserve heretical status.

[3] These concepts are outlined by Augustine in nat. et. gr. 2, 6, 7, 10, 20, 21, 47, 58.

attacked these views so fiercely that the Pelagians were eventually excommunicated as heretics.[4] Yet there remains doubt as to whether Pelagius himself actually taught what was attributed to him. In fact, the pejorative term "Pelagian" became the favorite accusation at that time (a theological death sentence) against any person teaching a doctrine another Christian bishop might oppose.[5]

A. Infant Baptism

One critical question remained throughout the conflict with the Pelagians. Why did the church practice the tradition of baptizing infants? Tertullian had spoken out against infant baptism over two-hundred years earlier, pointing out that the child should wait until he or she was old enough to make his or her own decision.[6] About 405 CE, Augustine admitted that he did not know why infant baptism was practiced.[7] For twenty-five years Augustine was solidly within traditional Christian doctrine of the first four centuries fighting the Stoics, Gnostics, and Manichaeans by teaching that God's foreknowledge

---

[4] Innocent responded to Epistle 176 from the Council of Milevis with excommunication of Caelestius and Pelagius.

[5] Bonner, *The Myth of Pelagianism*.

[6] Tertullian, (*De bapt.*18): "The Lord said, 'Do not prohibit them to come to me.' Therefore, let them come while adolescents, let them 'come' while they are learning, while learning where to come; let them become Christians when they have become able to know Christ! Why does the innocent age rush to the remission of sins?"

[7] Augustine, *an.quant.*80: "In this context, also, how much benefit is there in the consecration of infant children? It is a most difficult (obscure) question. However, that some benefit exists is to be believed. Reason will discover this when it should be asked."

of human free choice determined his election of persons.[8] But this all changed in 412 CE. The major theological conflict with Pelagius caused him to rethink this tradition and converted him to his later DUPIED.[9]

His reasoning started with church tradition then logically progressed in this manner:

1.) The church baptizes infants.

2.) Water baptism is for forgiveness of sin and reception of the Holy Spirit.

3.) Some dying infants are rushed by their Christian parents to the bishop for baptism but die before this can occur, while other infants born of prostitutes are abandoned on the streets when a church virgin rushes them to the bishop who baptizes them.

4.) These infants have no control over whether or not they are baptized and receive the Holy Spirit to become Christians.

5.) Therefore, God must unilaterally and unconditionally predetermine which infants are damned and which are justified. Augustine eventually taught even when "ministers prepared for giving baptism to the infants, it still is not given, because God does not choose" (*Persev.* 31). Therefore, logically, God's election must be unconditional since infants have no

---

[8] James Swindal and Harry Gensler, *The Sheed and Ward Anthology of Catholic Philosophy* (Lewiston, NY: Sheed and Ward, 2005), 39–40. Swindal and Gensler admit that patristic thinkers embraced human free will, but somehow they miss that the later Augustine refuted what the saints, bishops, and presbyters since Justin Martyr and Irenaeus had championed. This occurs despite their admission that Manichaeism's parent, Gnosticism, "combined biblical, Neoplatonic, and Persian elements."

[9] Wilson, *Augustine's Conversion*; See also Henry Chadwick, *Early Christian Thought and the Classical Tradition* (Oxford: At the Clarendon Press, 1966), 110–11.

personal sin, no merit, no good works, and no choice.

Because infants have no personal sin, he deduced their baptisms for forgiveness of sin must be based upon their inherited guilt (*reatus*) from Adam's first sin. No prior author taught infants were guilty and damned from Adam's sin and required water baptism for salvation.[10] Newborns were not guilty of Adam's sin but suffered consequences from Adam's sin. For comparison, a child of a prison inmate is not guilty of the crime but suffers because of that crime. God rebuked Job's friends for teaching this theology in the book of Job.[11] Augustine's theodicy (a defense vindicating God for apparent evil) also demanded that every punishment, pain, and loss in a person's life be justly deserved for sin for that individual due to his Stoic Providential micromanagement.[12] If infants die, then they must be personally guilty and be damned for that guilt of sin. This is called direct retribution theology. Not many theologians agree with this view. In fact, even Augustine admits:

---

[10] This included Augustine's mentor Ambrose who held the traditional view of inherited sin propensity within the physical body but without *reatus* (guilt, crime, fault) whereas Ambrose and others had used the milder *culpa* (imperfection, wrong-doing, sin, error). Henry Chadwick, *Saint Ambrose: On the Sacraments*, The Latin Text (London: Mowbray and Co., 1960; reprint, Chicago, IL: Loyola University Press, 1961), 74, fnt.3 and 136, fnt.6. See Ambrose's *de Poenitentia*, 1, *Ep.* 41.7, and *de Mysteriis* 6. Cf., Wilson, *Augustine's Conversion*; *Oxford Latin Dictionary*, s.v, "*reatus*" and "*culpa*"; *Dictionary of Ecclesiastical Latin*, s.v. "*reatus*" and "*culpa.*"

[11] A person suffering hardship, pain, or disasters must have sinned and God is punishing him (per Job's "friends").

[12] Chadwick, *Augustine*, 109.

I am myself keenly aware of how problematic this question is, and I recognize that my powers are not sufficient to get to the bottom of it. Here too I like to exclaim with Paul, *Oh the depths of the riches!* (Rom. 11:33). Unbaptized infants go to damnation; they are like the apostles words, after all: *From one to condemnation* (Rom. 5:16). I cannot find a satisfactory and worthy explanation... [he cites all of Rom.11:33–36] (*s.*294.7).[13]

Augustine could truthfully claim that he was not teaching Manichaeism because he invented a subtle distinction. Manichaeans eternally damned newborns based upon created nature (physical matter was evil). Augustine eternally damned newborns based on fallen nature (Adam's sin). This way Augustine attempted to spare the Christian God the shocking accusation Augustine himself had made against the Manichaeans of damning newborns who he created with an evil nature incapable of good (*Faust.* 22.22). But in Augustine's Stoic Providence, God had ordained Adam to sin resulting in a fallen nature incapable of choosing good. So whether by created nature or fallen nature, newborn humans were still damned by nature—damned without any personal choice as to their eternal abodes. These changes are Augustine's first steps with "T" of total depravity and the "U" of Unconditional election in modern Calvinism's TULIP. Not even one prior Christian author taught this theology.

B. Stoic and Manichaean Philosophies

Augustine brought into Christianity the Manichaean concepts of total inability (infants cannot make a choice), damnable sin at birth, and unconditional election (God chooses unilaterally). This logical deduction

---

[13] Edmund Hill, O.P., *The Works of Saint Augustine: A New Translation for the 21st Century*, Sermons III/8, Sermon 294 (Hyde Park, NY: New City Press, 1994), 184. Augustine reverses the apostle Paul's exclamatory praise for God's undeserved mercy into praise for his [Manichaean] God's undeserved eternal damnation of innocent infants!

from infants being baptized was then extrapolated to adult humans—human choice was unnecessary. Note that the basis for this logical argument was the assumed salvific power of water baptism for an infant combined with the Stoic philosophy of divine meticulous control of all events. We do not possess even one prior extant Christian writing that taught these three pagan ideas.

Augustine admitted he had abandoned the centuries-old Christian doctrine of human free choice.[14] "In the solution of this question I struggled in behalf of free choice of the will, but the grace of God won out." (*Retr.* 2.1). "When I began my books on Free Choice [3.68]... I still doubted the condemnation of infants not born again [baptized]" (*pers.*30) and "before this heresy [Pelagianism] arose, they did not have the necessity to deal with this question, so difficult of solution. They would have undoubtedly have done so if they had been compelled to respond to such men." (*pers.*2.4; *pred.*44). The famous scholar Pelikan appropriately lamented Augustine's rejection of traditional Christian theology and Augustine's feeble excuse for doing so.[15]

---

[14] William Babcock, s.v. "Sin" in *The Encyclopedia of Early Christianity*, 2nd edn., Everett Ferguson, ed. (New York, NY: Routledge, 1998): "It could also be represented by speaking—as Augustine did, in what was a significant break with the previous tradition—of the impairment of the human will and the vitiation of human nature, after Adam's sin, with the result that human beings, on their own, are no longer capable of willing and doing the good (*Nat. et Grat.* and the anti-Pelagian writings...)."

[15] Jaroslav Pelikan, *The Christian Tradition: A History of the Development of Doctrine*, vol. 1 (Chicago, IL: University of Chicago Press, 1971–1989), 278–280, esp. 280.

Augustine attempted to use "divine persuasion"[16] as his means to avoid rejecting the free will defense of all prior Christian authors against Stoicism and Manichaeism. Of the extant writings of authors who taught on the topic, over fifty from 95 CE through 412 CE supported and defended this Christian view of free choice against the Stoics, Gnostics, and Manichaeans.[17] For

---

[16] Persuasion is not possible. A dead will cannot be persuaded. It must be unilaterally awakened from the dead. Augustine struggles to keep his innovations within Christian teachings.

[17] Ibid. In addition to all of the primary sources listed in my thesis, see also Hall (1979), 42; Glenn Hinson, "Justin Martyr" and "Irenaeus," in Lindsay Jones, ed. *Encyclopedia of Religion*, 2nd edn. (2005), 5043–5045 and 4538–4541; Antonio Orbe, *Antropologia de San Ireneo* (Madrid: Biblioteca de Autores Cristianos, 1969), 296–7; Bernard Sesboüé, „Irenäus von Lyon: Mann der Kirche und Lehrer der Kirche," in Johannes Arnold, Rainer Berndt SJ, and Ralf Stammberger, eds. *Väter der Kirche Ekklesiales Denken von den Anfängen bis in die Neuzeit* (Zürich: Ferdinand Schöningh, 2004), 105; William Floyd, *Clement of Alexandria's Treatment of the Problem of Evil* (Oxford: Oxford University Press, 1971), 28 (cf., *Strom.*1.34, 6.4, 6.7); Eric Osborne, *Tertullian, First Theologian of the West* (Cambridge: Cambridge University Press, 1997), 100; Joseph O'Leary, "Grace," in John McGuckin, ed. *The Westminster Handbook to Origen* (Louisville, KY: Westminster John Knox Press, 2004), 115 (cf., *C.Cels.*6.55); McIntire (2005), "Free Will and Predestination: Christian Concepts"; Williams (1927), 297; John N.D. Kelly, *Early Christian Doctrines* (New York, NY: Harper and Row, 1960; repr. London: Continuum, 2004), 149; Verna Harrison, *Grace and Human Freedom According to St. Gregory of Nyssa* (Lampeter: Edwin Mellen Press, 1992), 130–31; Martin Streck, *Das schönste Gut: Der menschliche Wille bei Nemesius von Emesa und Gregor von Nyssa* (Göttingen: Vandenhoeck and Ruprecht, 2005), 173,180–82; Moxon (1922), 40; Henry Chadwick, *Saint Ambrose: On the Sacraments*, The Latin Text (London: Mowbray and Co., 1960; repr. Chicago: Loyola University Press, 1960), 136, fnt.6; Blowers (1999), "Original Sin."

them, God's election was according to God's foreknowledge (cf., 1 Pet. 1:2),[18] as Augustine himself had taught for decades.[19] To avoid violating centuries of Christian teaching about free will, Augustine simply redefined free will. He concluded that God must micromanage and manipulate the circumstances that would guarantee a person would "freely" respond to the invitation of God's calling to eternal life.[20] Now, his God had to give faith and regeneration to free the will (a "freed will") so humans could choose the good. His new God also divinely arranged circumstances to assure his elect would respond correctly to his grace. A millennium later, Calvinists would refer to this as Irresistible grace, the "I" in TULIP.

Long before Augustine lived, the Roman statesman Cicero (*ca.*50 BCE)

---

[18] Note the bias of BDAG (3rd edn.) in considering κατά in verse 3 as meaning "because of" without admitting this in the κατά of the immediately preceding verse (v.2). *A Greek-English Lexicon of the New Testament and Other Early Christian Literature*, Third edition, rev. and ed. by Frederick Danker (Chicago, IL: University of Chicago Press, 2000), κατά. B.a.5.δ. "Oft. the norm is at the same time the reason, so that *in accordance with* and *because of* are merged:...**1 Pt 1.3.**"

[19] Wetzel, "Simplicianum, Ad": "As late as the first part of *Ad Simplicianum*, Augustine rests secure in his belief that it remains to a person's free choice to seek the aid of the divine liberator, regardless of how debilitating addiction to sin has become (1.1.14)" Cf., Lenka Karfíková, *Grace and the Will according to Augustine* (Leiden: Brill, 2012), 7-61; Brown, *Augustine of Hippo,* 141–2; Marianne Djuth, "Will," in Allan D. Fitzgerald, ed. *Augustine Through the Ages: An Encyclopedia* (Grand Rapids, MI: Eerdmans, 1999), 883; Augustine, *83Div.Q* 68.3 and *Gen.c.Man.*1.6.

[20] Patout Burns, "From Persuasion to Predestination: Augustine on Freedom in Rational Creatures" in P. Blowers, et al., eds. In *Dominico Elquio, in Lordly Eloquence: Essays on Patristic Exegesis in Honour of Robert Louis Wilken* (Cambridge: Eerdmans, 2002), 307.

and numerous philosophers had argued that divine foreknowledge and human free will were incompatible. They cannot co-exist. But Augustine refuted this (*ciu.*5) claiming divine foreknowledge of the future occurs because God had pre-determined everything both good and bad (*ordo*), a concept common in Stoicism but absent in Cicero's Platonic philosophy (*On Divination*) and Christianity. Augustine now teaches "God foreordains human wills."[21] But Origin (*ca.*250) had clearly differentiated the Christian God's foreknowledge from the prior pagan divine foreknowledge—God's foreknowledge is not causative (*Com.Rom.*7.8.7). This vital distinction allows human free choice.

C. The Gift of Perseverance and Discriminatory Propitiation

Another novel doctrine emerged many years later—perseverance of the saints. Some baptized infants would become godly adult Christians while other baptized infants would fall away from the faith and live immoral lives. Since both infants possessed the Holy Spirit by baptism, what could explain the difference? Augustine concluded (logically, in his system) that God must give a second gift of grace called perseverance. God gives the gift of perseverance to only a few baptized infants.[22] Without this second gift of grace a baptized Christian with the Holy Spirit cannot persevere and ultimately will not be saved.[23]

---

[21] Christopher Kirwan, *Augustine* in The Arguments of the Philosophers (New York, NY: Routledge, 1989), 98–103.

[22] Augustine, (*persev.*1, 9–12, 21, 41); Peter Burnell, *The Augustinian Person* (Washington, DC: The Catholic University of America Press, 2005), 85–86.

[23] Augustine, *corrept.*18.

In modern Calvinism, this is the "P" of Perseverance of the saints. But notice that this perseverance differs significantly from Augustine's theology: for him, not all true Christians persevered in faith and good works. For Augustine, baptized babies who received the Holy Spirit and were regenerated could fall away if God did not give the second gift of perseverance. His logical invention of the second gift of perseverance was created for the very purpose of explaining this problem of Christians who did not persevere despite having the Holy Spirit.

This in turn led to another doctrinal change. Back in 411 CE, Augustine held to the traditional Christian doctrine on the "atonement" (propitiation)—that God loved and Christ died for the whole world. "Who indeed can doubt that in the term *world* all persons are indicated who enter the world by being born?" (*Pecc. merit.*1.26; cf., *conf.*6.7-8). But after incorporating his Gnostic Manichaeism into Christianity, Augustine attempted at least five answers over a decade of time trying to explain 1 Tim. 2:4—"who desires all men to be saved and to come to the knowledge of the truth"—on the extent of Christ's redeeming sacrifice.[24] His major premise was the pagan idea that God receives everything he desires. This is a variant of the philosophical

---

[24] Alexander Hwang, "Augustine's Various Interpretations of 1 Tim. 2: 4," *St.Patr.*43 (2006), 137–42.

mistake known as the "McEar error."[25] Augustine now teaches this error: Omnipotence (Stoic and Neoplatonic) is doing whatever the One desires. This ensures everything that occurs is exactly the Almighty's will and therefore must inevitably occur (*s*.214.4).[26] He concluded (logically) that because God gets everything he wants, God cannot desire all persons to be saved. If God desired it, every human would be saved. The Oxford Patristics expert Chadwick concluded that because Augustine's God does not desire it and refuses to save all persons, Augustine elevated God's sovereignty as absolute and God's justice was trampled.[27] The Christian God of love and equal justice

---

[25] The McEar error may have been first explained by William of Ockham (*ca.* 1340) against the inadequate or problematic definition of the word 'omnipotence.' Augustine's earlier variant of the error concludes that omnipotence necessarily results in God receiving everything He desires. See Leftow (2009), 168, where he exposes this McEar error from Augustine's "will" element; cf., John Rist, *Augustine: Ancient Thought Baptized* (Cambridge: Cambridge University Press, 1994), 272, 286; Richard La Croix. "The impossibility of defining 'omnipotence'." *Philosophical Studies* 32.2 (1977): 181–190; Alvin Plantinga. *God and other minds: a study of the rational justification of belief in God* (Ithaca, NY: Cornell University Press, 1967), 170; Edward Wierenga, "Omnipotence defined," *Philosophy and Phenomenological Research* 43.3 (1983): 363–-375 and *The Nature of God: An Inquiry into Divine Attributes* in Cornell Studies in the Philosophy of Religion (Ithaca, NY: Cornell University Press, 2003), Chapter 1.

[26] Augustine, (*symb.*2): "He does whatever He wills: that itself is omnipotence [by definition]. He does whatever He wishes well, whatever He wishes justly, but, whatever is evil, He does not will. No one resists the Omnipotent and not do what God wills."

[27] Henry Chadwick, "Freedom and Necessity in Early Christian Thought About God" in David Tracy and Nicholas Lash, eds. *Cosmology and Theology*. (Edinburgh: T & T Clark Ltd, 1983), 8–13.

was replaced by a Stoic God consumed solely with absolute power. Since this Stoic God does not waste causation or energy, this also logically demanded that Christ could not have died for those persons who would never be saved. Therefore, Christ must have died only for the elect since God does not waste causation or energy.[28]

This is the "L" in Limited atonement of Calvinism's TULIP. Christ did not die for the sins of the whole world but only for all of the elect around the whole world. Prior authors taught Christ died for every person in the world but only those elect who believed in Christ had their sins forgiven.

Finally, for the first time in his massive corpus, Augustine claims a Christian's perseverance in faith and good works is God's gift (*corrept.*10). He reaches this final conclusion by removing 1 Cor. 4:7 from its context.[29] In *corrept.*16, he first posits that all the "true elect" inevitably persevere. Therefore, a person can be genuinely regenerated and receive the Holy Spirit but be damned to Hell by not receiving the additional necessary gift of perseverance from God (*corrept.*18). Ironically, he himself astutely exclaims this is stupefying. Augustine also reverts to the Gnostic/Manichaean interpretation of Romans 11:33. He then conscripts Phil. 1:6 as a proof-text completely out of context of Paul's confidence that the Philippians will continue their

---

[28] See Donato Ogliari, *Gratia et Certamen: The Relationship between Grace and Free Will in the Discussion of Augustine with the so-called Semipelagian*s (Leuven: University Press, 2003).

[29] By asking, "And what do you have that you did not receive?" Paul rebukes prideful boasting in human abilities that created rivalries instead of crediting spiritual gifts to God who gave them. Cf., John Barclay, "1 Corinthians" in *The Oxford Bible Commentary*, John Barton and John Muddiman, eds. (Oxford: Oxford University Press, 2001), 1115. Augustine reverts to Gnostic Manichaeism—God regenerates human by giving initial faith.

partnership/fellowship in the gospel through their financial contributions to him.[30] Despite this contextual abuse of Phil. 1:6, he proclaims, "by this gift they cannot fail to persevere" (*corrept.*34). This erroneous proof-text was the basis for proving Augustine's newly discovered divine "gift of perseverance." The TULIP of Augustinian-Calvinism is complete.

D. Conclusion

For Augustine, "Providence" allows or actively prevents infant baptism resulting in salvation for newborns who lack any "will" or choice. This required Augustine to reinterpret infant baptism as salvific from eternal damnation at birth from a mistranslation of Romans 5:12. It also required him to resurrect the Manichaean interpretation of spiritual damnation due to physical birth and revise it into inherited damnation from Adam's sin.

Augustine converted from traditional Christian free choice to pagan Divine Unilateral Predetermination of Individuals' Eternal Destinies (DUPIED). Since infants have no "wills" and no faith, it is the parents' faith that saves them at baptism (eternal salvation by proxy). God unilaterally determines who will be granted salvation and who will be denied salvation, either by directly intervening to successfully bring the infant to the bishop, or by actively blocking that infant's access to the baptismal font. Infant baptism for salvation from eternal damnation and Stoic Providence in aiding or

---

[30] David Black, *Linguistics for Students of New Testament Greek*, 2nd edn. (Grand Rapids, MI: Baker Books, 1995), 177–8. Compare Phil. 4:10–20 where the concluding good work of financial support matches the beginning Phil. 1:5 of fellowship in the gospel that Paul is confident will continue. Nothing suggests eternal life or perseverance.

blocking that baptism were the foundational building blocks for his novel theology.

Once Augustine borrowed total depravity (T, inability to respond) and unconditional election (U, no human choice allowed) from his prior religious and philosophical compatriots, the remainder of his TULIP progressed logically. It should astound us to realize how Augustine's novel theology was birthed. Irresistible grace was a Manichaean doctrine. He invented the gift of perseverance as a second gift of God to explain the problem of lapsed Christians. In his theology, perseverance was never guaranteed for every "true" Christian. God no longer loved every human enough for Christ to die on their behalf—like the Manichaeans, now God only loved the elect. With his novel (for Christianity) theology complete, we can now explore the scriptures Augustine used in his defense of this TULIP theology.

Chapter 5
Augustine Reverted to Manichaean Interpretations of Scripture

Augustine used Christian scriptures to prove his new doctrines. But unfortunately, he used Manichaean interpretations—the very interpretations he had previously refuted as heretical after becoming a Christian. He now converts back to his Manichaean truths.

A. Manichaean Deterministic Interpretations

The Gnostic Manichaeans cited John 6:65, 14:6, and Ephesians 2:1–9 as proof-texts for unconditional election against Christian free choice. Fortunatus the Manichaean had quoted Eph. 2:8–9 as evidence for initial faith being God's gift by grace (DUPIED).[1] But Augustine had previously correctly attacked this error: "I say it is not sin, if it be not committed by one's own will; hence also there is reward, because of our own will we do right" (*c.Fort.*21).

Such pagan ideas had been refuted by Augustine until 412 CE when he readopted the Manichaean interpretations against all prior Christian authors. Psalm 51:5 had never been cited by a Christian author as proof of separation from God at physical birth (a Manichaean doctrine) until Augustine used it to turn traditional original sin (sin propensity, moral weakness, and physical

---

[1] The first extant "Christian" writing claiming faith itself was a gift of God instead of a human response was from the gnostic Basilides who was refuted by Clement of Alexandria *ca.*190 (*Strom.*2.3–4; cp., *Strom.*4.11, *Quis Dives Salvetur*, 10).

death) into Augustinian original sin (inherited sin and guilt from Adam pro-
ducing damnation at birth and total spiritual inability).[2]

In 395 CE, he held the traditional view of Romans 5:12, "Therefore as sin
came into the world through one man and death through sin, and so death
spread to all men because all men sinned" (RSV). This allowed him to omit
Rom. 5:12 as unimportant in his commentary on Romans. It was unnecessary
to comment. In fact, his book *On Free Will* claims:

> But we also use it in speaking of the nature with which we are born mortal,
> ignorant and subject to the flesh, which is really the penalty of sin. In this sense
> the apostle says: "We also were by nature children of wrath even as others."
> [55]... But if any of Adam's race should be willing to turn to God, and so
> overcome the punishment which had been merited by the original turning away
> from God, it was fitting not only that he should not be hindered but that he
> should also receive divine aid. In this way also the Creator showed how easily
> man might have retained, if he had so willed, the nature with which he was
> created, because his offspring had power to transcend that in which he was
> born. (*De Libero Arbitrio* 3.54–55)[3]

After 411 CE, his Manichaean view of inherited birth guilt and his Stoic view
of micromanaging Providence pervaded his theology with infants being

---

[2] Ps. 51:5 is hyperbole as seen by comparing Ps. 58:3. "The wicked go astray
from the womb, they err from their birth, speaking lies" (RSV). Newborns cannot
speak lies—they cannot speak. Origen specifically cited but denied any guilt for sin
at birth in Ps. 51 when combating pagans and Gnostics (*C.Cels.*7.50) although he
teaches the sin nature (*genuinae sordes peccati*) enters through physical birth
(*Hom.Lev.*8.3, 12.4; *Com.Rom.*5.9; *C.Cels.*7.50). Cf., Wilson, *Augustine's Conversion*, 311–16, where Horace (whose works Augustine had read, *c.mend.*28; *s.*2.6;
*ep.*1.7), utilized hyperbole to express the pervasiveness of human vices, particularly
as beginning from birth (*Serm.Q.Hoarti Flacci* 1.68: «nam vitiis nemo sine nasci-
tur», "For nobody is born without vices/faults." Early Christians had likewise used
Ps. 51:4 to demonstrate human depravity but not total depravity (inability to respond
to God from inherited guilt and loss of free will).

[3] Note this section 3.55 was original and not revised by Augustine since the revision stopped at 3.54

damned at birth by divine unilateral choice (*Pecc.mer.* 1.29-30).[4]

But there was a problem: Christianity required personal faith for baptismal regeneration. So Augustine utilized an approach combining Stoic determinism and Christian doctrine. He invented a proxy salvation whereby one person can believe for another, so that the infant being baptized need not believe in Christ. "There is not indeed a man among the faithful, who would hesitate to call such infants believers merely from the circumstance that such a designation is derived from the act of believing; for although incapable of such an act themselves, yet others are sponsors for them in the sacraments" (*Pecc.mer.* 1.38). Personal faith was no longer required.

> And so, even if that faith that is found in the will of believers does not make a little one a believer, the sacrament of the faith itself [baptism], nonetheless, now does so. For, just as the response is given that the little one believes, he is also in that sense called a believer, not because he assents to the reality with his mind, but because he receives the sacrament of that reality. (*ep.*98.10).[5]

The Augustinian scholar Bonner wrote, "It has been remarked that the number of texts to which Augustine appealed to establish this doctrine of Original Sin is remarkably limited: Ps.50:7 [51:5 EW]: Job 14:4-5: John 3:5; Ephesians 2:3; Romans 5:12."[6] These were enlisted as proof-texts after Augustine invented his new doctrine.

---

[4] Johannes van Oort, "Augustine on sexual concupiscence and original sin," *St.Patr.*22 (1989): 382–86.

[5] Translation by Roland Teske, S.J., *The Works of Saint Augustine: A Translation of the 21st Century*, Letters 1–99, II.1 (Hyde Park, NY: New City Press, 2001), 432.

[6] Gerald Bonner, "Augustine, the Bible and the Pelagians," in Pamela Bright, editor and translator. *Augustine and the Bible* (Notre Dame, IN: University of Notre Dame Press, 1999) 231–232.

B. John 3:5 and Romans 5:12

"Jesus answered, 'Truly, truly, I say to you, unless one is born of water and the Spirit, he cannot enter the kingdom of God.'" (John 3:5, RSV). This verse became his essential foundation, eventually using it as his first scriptural defense for salvific infant water baptism in 420 CE (*Nat. orig.*1.1). Prior to this change, Augustine had taught baptism was not required for salvation for the thief on the cross since faith was salvific. "Baptism was credited to the believing thief, and what could not be received in a crucified body was rendered acceptable in an unshackled soul, so likewise the Holy Spirit was given in a hidden way before the Lord's glorification" (*Div. quaest.*62). Similarly, in about 400 CE in *Bapt.*4.10 he writes, "'Faith comes from the heart for righteousness, but confession is made with the mouth for salvation' [Rom 10:10]—is evident in that thief even apart from the visible sacrament of baptism." The elder Augustine had to retract his earlier teaching as erroneous (*Retract.*1.26) since it contradicted his post-411 CE requirement of water baptism to remove the damnable *reatus* (guilt) of concupiscence (the sin propensity) inherited from Adam. To save himself from embarrassment and establish his new requirement for water baptism, he dreamed up the thief was "baptized" when Christ's own water and blood from the spear strike splashed.

Yet, the Catholic scholar Redmond doubts the legitimacy of Augustine's interpretation of John 3:5 as water baptism.[7] Furthermore, the Catholic Augustinian scholar Hill exposes the problem in this logic, "babies who die unbaptized therefore go to hell. Augustine assumed that baptism was the only means of liberating grace available to them. And it is precisely this assumption that renders his whole argument weak, and his conclusion highly questionable."[8]

Romans 5:12 was critical: "Therefore as sin came into the world through one man and death through sin, and so death spread to all men because all men sinned" (RSV). The scholarly literature contains numerous discussions of the Latin mistranslation of Rom. 5:12 "as in whom all sinned" (*in quo*), versus NT Greek "because all sinned" (ἐφ' ᾧ).[9] If all people sinned in Adam

---

[7] Richard Redmond, "Infant Baptism: History and Pastoral Problems," *Theological Studies* 30 (March 1969): 79–89, esp. 84: "For, as Raymond Brown says, John's concern here is one of contrasting flesh and spirit....The negative universal of this verse, then, does not prove the necessity of infant baptism. Nor do we find any '*quamprimum*' urgency about baptism, since for a long time in Rome Easter and Pentecost were the only dates for baptism." The context clarifies the physical birth versus spiritual birth with the mother's "water breaking" being the common terminology for a physical birth even in our modern time. The context is not water baptism.

[8] Edmund Hill, O.P., *The Works of Saint Augustine* (Sermon 294), 196.

[9] Bruce Harbert, "Romans 5:12: Old Latin and Vulgate in the Pelagian Controversy," *St.Patr.*22 (1989), 262; Philip Quinn, "Sin" in *Routledge Encyclopedia of Philosophy* (London: Routledge, 1998); G. Vandervelde, *Original Sin: Two Major Trends in Contemporary Roman Catholic Reinterpretation* (Amsterdam: Rodopi N.V., 1975), 22; David Weaver, "From Paul to Augustine: Romans 5:12 in Early Christian Exegesis," *St. Vladimir's Theological Quarterly* 27.3 (1983); Kelly, *Early Christian Doctrines*, 2nd edn., 181–2; Bradley Nassif, "Toward a 'catholic' Understanding of St. Augustine's View of Original Sin," *Union Seminary Quarterly*

(in whom) then all people are guilty at birth.[10] But Augustine did not know Greek until later in his life.[11] He upheld this mistranslation as his definitive proof after inventing his Manichaean-Christian doctrine of separation from God at birth with all humanity damned by guilt from Adam's sin.[12] Traditional original sin with *physical* death *because* (ἐφ' ᾧ, because) all sin now became Augustinian original sin with *spiritual* death from Adam *in whom* all sinned (*in quo*, in whom).[13] So the traditional interpretation that all die *physically* as a consequence of Adam's sin transformed into the Manichaean-Augustinian view that all sinned in Adam, so every human is therefore spiritually dead, guilty, and damned at birth.

C. 1 Timothy 2:4

Augustine cites 1 Tim. 2:4 only once prior to 412 CE: "God our Savior, who desires all men to be saved and to come to the knowledge of the truth." (1 Tim.

Review 39.4 (1984), 287–299, esp. 296; F.L. Cross and E.A. Livingstone, s.v., "Original Sin" in *The Oxford Dictionary of the Christian Church*, 3rd edn. (Oxford: Oxford University Press, 2005).

[10] See Wilson, *Augustine's Conversion* for a more detailed explanation.

[11] Augustine admits his poor knowledge of Greek (*c. litt. Pet.* 2.91), interpreted disparately but which can be ascertained as he chronologically improves his knowledge from *ca.*400 through the next decades (*PL* 43, 292).

[12] William Mann, "Augustine on Evil and Original Sin," in *The Cambridge Companion to Augustine*, ed. Eleanore Stump and Norman Kretzmann (Cambridge, UK: Normal Publication, 2001), 47; Anthony Padovano, *Original Sin and Christian Anthropology* (Washington, DC: Corpus Books, 1967), 11.

[13] George Vandervelde,. *Original Sin: Two Major Trends in Contemporary Roman Catholic Reinterpretation*. Amsterdam: Rodopi N.V., 1975), 5. See Wilson, *Augustine's Conversion* for a more detailed explanation.

2:3b–4, RSV).[14] Allegedly, the Pelagians assumed 1 Tim. 2:4 taught that God gave faith to all persons. Augustine easily refuted their error by changing the text from "God wills" to God "provides opportunity" (*Spir. et litt.*37–38). So God does not really desire the salvation of every human, he merely provides different (unequal) opportunities. Not until 414 CE (*ep.*149) does 'all' people change to mean 'all kinds/classes' of people, and *S.*304.2 (417 CE) repeats this concept. Only in 421 CE (*C. Jul.*4.8.42) did Augustine alter the text to mean 'all who are saved' are saved by God's will, which he repeats the next year (*Enchir.*97, 103). Many people cannot be saved: "many are not saved because God does not will this" (*ep.*217.19). Unbelievably, Augustine claims God makes Christians desire the salvation of those whom he has damned (*Corrept.*15, 47). Rist adeptly identifies this as "the most pathetic passage."[15] By 429 CE, Augustine quotes 1 Cor. 1:18 (but he adds the word *such* to 1 Tim. 2:4, "all such men"), then redefines *all* as *all those elected*, thereby implying an irresistible call of God. Over a twenty year period Augustine attempts five different explanations of this text. Thus, Hwang's analysis of Augustine's evolving interpretations of 1 Tim. 2:4 correctly concludes,

> Then the radical shift occurred, brought about by the open and heated conflict with the Pelagians. 'Desires' took on absolute and efficacious qualities, and the meaning of 'all' was reduced to the predestined. 1 Tim. 2:4 should be understood, then, as meaning that God saves only the predestined. All others, apparently, do not even have a prayer.[16]

---

[14] *Exp. quaest. Rom.*74. He compares it with masters in Eph. 6:6., possibly restricting 'all' to authorities.

[15] John Rist, "Augustine on Free Will and Predestination," in Robert Markus, ed. *Augustine: A Collection of Critical Essays* (New York, NY: Doubleday, 1972), 239.

[16] Hwang (2003), 137–142.

D. John 14:6 and 6:65

Fortunatus the Manichaean also cited John 14:6 to prove unilateral determinism, "No one can come to the Father except through me," since "He chose
souls worthy of himself for his own holy will ... and were imbued with a
faith" (*Fort*.3). Augustine defended the Christian view by mocking the Manichaean god: "corrupted and worn out I have lost my free choice. You know
the necessity that has pressed me down. Why do you blame me for the
wounds I received?" (cf., *S.*12.5, *S.*100.3).

Augustine does not cite these verses until after 412 CE when he uses the
Manichaean interpretations to prove his new total inability/incapacity for human faith (*Grat*.10, *C. du. ep. Pel*.4.13–16, *ep*.186.38).

E. Psalm 51:5

"Behold, I was brought forth in iniquity, and in sin did my mother conceive
me" Psalm 51:5 (RSV). This text was cited by numerous prior Christians in
the traditional Christian sense of inevitable human sinfulness. Before 412
CE, Augustine cited it similarly (e.g., *Conf.*1.7; *Enar. Ps.*51.10). His early
use follows the Jewish and early Christian interpretation that "(Ps.51:7;
50:7), merely means that everyone born of a woman becomes a sinner in this
world, without fail."[17] Augustine's more Manichaean interpretation (babies
are born damned from Adam's sin) first appears in 412 CE in *Pecc. merit.*1.34
and 3.13 (alongside Job 14:4 supporting infant baptism and infant participa-
tion in the Eucharist). Thereafter he utilizes this proof-text constantly (*Grat.
Chr.*2.47, *Nupt. et conc.* 2.50, *C. du. ep. Pel.*4.4, *Gen. litt.*6.15, and

---

[17] Herbert Haag, *Biblische Schopfungslehre und kirchliche Ersundenlehre.*
Stuttgart: Katho-lisches Bibelwerk, 1966. *Is Original Sin in Scripture?* Translated
by Dorothy Thompson (New York, NY: Sheed and Ward, 1969), 106.

*Enchir.*46), multiplying in *C. Jul.* with five occurrences (1.9, 32 and 2.4, 5, 15) and seven in *C. Jul. imp.* (1.52, 59; 2.73; 3.110; 4.82, 90; 6.14).

F. Ephesians 2:3 and 2:8–9

"Among these we all once lived in the passions of our flesh, following the desires of body and mind, and so we were by nature children of wrath, like the rest of mankind. . . . For by grace you have been saved through faith; and this is not your own doing, it is the gift of God—not because of works, lest any man should boast" Ephesians 2:3, 8–9 (RSV). When Fortunatus the Manichaean cited Eph. 2:3 and 2:8–10 as proof-texts for Gnostic-type determinism, Augustine disagreed, rebutting that it "clearly reveals free choice" (*Fort.*17). Augustine argued the context of Eph. 2:1–3 concerned personal sins and not damnation by nature. "Remember that the apostle said that we were alienated from God by our way of life." (*Fort.*18). For the early Augustine, the object of God's wrath was not human nature by birth but through personal sin, which he proved by Eph. 2:2 "in which you once walked." After 412 CE, Augustine reverts to Fortunatas' Manichaean view: "So both the twins were born *by nature children of wrath* [Eph. 2:3]" (*Enchir.*98). As expected, *Pecc. merit.* 1.29, 46 (cf., 2.15) introduces this verse as a proof text after which it consistently buttresses his inherited inborn total incapacity claim (*Nat. grat.*3, 81; *Perf.*3; *Grat. Chr.*1.55; *Nupt. et conc.*2.20; *C. du. ep. Pel.* 1.15, 3.4; *Fid. symb.*23; *C. Jul.*2.28, 3.33, 3.78; *Gen. litt.*9.17,10.21; *Enchir.*33, 98; *Cur.*2; *C. Jul. imp.*2.228, 3.11, 3.79, 4.124, 5.22). Augustine now (after 411 CE) views babies as born under wrath and damnation inherited from Adam's sin with no ability to respond to God as grown adults.

In 413 CE during *Sermon* 294.14, Augustine first preached Eph. 2:3 with full Augustinian original sin (damnable guilt at birth). He abandons the prior traditional Christian view of Eph. 2:3 (nature corrupted from personal sin; cf., *S*.D29.12 and *S*.400.5) for the Manichaean view of nature damned at birth. But he cleverly nuanced this as "born" rather than "created" so as not to be accused of teaching Manichaeism's damnation by created nature.

Fortunatus also quoted Eph. 2:8–9 as definitive proof for initial faith as being God's gift by grace (*Fort*.16). Augustine objected (*Fort*.16–17). He never mentioned faith as God's gift when citing Eph. 2:8–9 (e.g., *Virginit*.41, *S*.212.1) until after 411 CE.[18] Its first appearance where Augustine defends the Manichaean interpretation occurs in *Spir. et litt*.56 (412 CE) where he builds upon his work immediately prior (*Pecc. mer.*). He claims since it is obviously impossible for newborns to have faith or believe (they cannot yet understand to make a choice) then God gives newborns salvation through the parents' faith. He now teaches proxy salvation. The faith of someone else can save you. The critical foundation of infant baptism for salvation in Augustine's novel theology cannot be overstated.

G. Conclusion

Augustine had earlier taunted the Manichaeans for inventing a god who damned persons eternally when those persons had no ability to do good or choose good (*Contra Faustas* 22.22). Augustine converted back to a Manichaean proof-text interpretation of Eph. 2:8 wherein God regenerated the dead will and infused faith (*gr.et.lib.arb*.17). Augustine reverts to his prior Manichaean training with their interpretations of multiple scriptures. Unbelievably, in his 412 CE conversion, Augustine accepted Fortunatus the Manichaean's DUPIED interpretation of John 14:6 (*gr.et.lib.arb*.3–4,10) and

---

[18] Since Augustine revised *Lib. arb*.3.47–54 and *Simpl*.2.6 after 412 CE these are not exceptions.

Eph. 2:8–9 (*Fort.*16–17). He now accepts and teaches the very interpretations he had previously refuted against Manichaeans. This scenario is precisely why early church policy forbade any prior Manichaean from becoming a Christian bishop and why charges of Manichaeism had been brought against the early Augustine before ordination. His many works against Manichaeism eventually (prematurely) convinced church leaders (against church policy) that Augustine's ordination as a bishop had been safely justified.

Chapter 6
Augustine Taught Determinism as Predestination

A. Gnostic and Manichaean Determinism

Prior to 250 CE, Gnostics and heretics had used scripture to justify their non-Christian doctrines. They quoted Christian scripture verses as proof of their deterministic DUPIED (*P.Arch.*3.1.18–21) such as Phil. 2:13, "for it is God who works in you, both to will and to work for his good pleasure." Gnostics also cited Romans 9:18–21.

> So then he has mercy on whomever he wills, and he hardens whomever he wills. You will say to me then, "Why does he still find fault? For who can resist his will?" But who are you, O man, to answer back to God? Will what is molded say to its molder, "Why have you made me like this?" Has the potter no right over the clay, to make out of the same lump one vessel for honorable use and another for dishonorable use? (Rom. 9:18–21, ESV)

Gnostics had used Romans 9–11 as their deterministic proof text by changing the context from nations and temporal benefits to a context of individual eternal destinies. Origen defended this text against Gnostic heretics (*P. Arch.*3.1.18, 21). Valentinus the "Gnostic Christian" had taught the message of salvation was offered to all, but only the elect (πνευματικοί, the spiritual ones who possessed Light particles) were empowered by God to accept the invitation and receive salvation (*Ev.Ver.*11, 30–31; *Corp.Herm.*1.26).[1] The Manichaean teachings, which were the theological pinnacle of Gnosticism,

---

[1] Albrecht Dihle, *The Theory of Will in Classical Antiquity* (Berkeley, CA: University of California Press, 1982), 151–4.

utilized these Gnostic ideas.

Yet no known major religion or philosophy has ever advertised itself as believing absolute determinism. Such a repugnant concept demands some accommodation for a "free will," even if it is disingenuous (bogus). This was precisely the manner in which Stoics, Gnostics, and Manichaeans presented their versions of determinism. Even Augustine himself had previously accused the Manichaeans of carrying about the carcass of "free will" gutted of its Christian meaning.[2]

B. Stoic and Neoplatonic Determinism

Genuine free choice and moral responsibility are inseparably linked—they require each other. Although some scholars categorize Stoics as compatibilists, the contradictory Stoic "fated free will" rejects this common sense approach. For Stoics, Fate controls every minute occurrence in the universe in

---

[2] Faculty members (and others) at both Oxford and Cambridge have sounded this warning: Tim Mawson, *Free Will: A Guide for the Perplexed* (London: The Continuum International Publishing Group, 2011); Linda Zagzebski, "Recent Work on Divine Foreknowledge and Free Will" in Robert Kane, ed., *The Oxford Handbook of Free Will* (Oxford: Oxford University Press, 2002), 45–64; Christopher Stead, *Philosophy in Christian Antiquity* (Cambridge: Cambridge University Press, 1994), 50–52; Eleonore Stump, "Augustine on free will" in Eleonore Stump and Norman Kretzman, eds. *The Cambridge Companion to Augustine* (Cambridge: Cambridge University Press, 2001), 142: "On the contrary, unless Augustine is willing to accept that God's giving of grace is responsive to something in human beings, even if that something is not good or worthy of merit, I don't see how he can be saved from the imputation of theological determinism with all its infelicitous consequences." These present an astute discussion of covert determinism masquerading as free will (what I call pseudocompatibilism).

a moral imperative (Cicero, *Div.*1, 125–6). Although the person had no possibility of acting on an opportunity, "free will" remains solely by definition (Cicero, *Fat.*12–15).[3] One scholar correctly clarifies that even the infamously deterministic Stoics, "took elaborate precautions to protect their system from rigid determinism."[4] They used clever nuances. Philo's *On Providence* appropriates a Stoic view. Another famous scholar states a reading of this treatise by itself would lead one to the conclusion that Philo was a determinist.[5] Winston identified Philo's view as a "relative free will theory taught by the Stoics, and often characterized as 'compatibilism'" but he concluded this was *not* a genuine free will (but rather what I term a "non-free free will" of Stoicism). Philo's Stoic view departed from more traditional varieties of Judaism.[6]

Likewise, Plotinus (the father of Neoplatonism) says he rejects an outward "Necessity" and posits the Stoic theory of freedom to do whatever we desire. However, at the same time he subjects humans to determinism since "the will" has been bound by innate universal wickedness (*Enn.*III,2.10). Evil produced a totally incapacitating fall, imprisoning us against our wills (*Enn.*I,8.5). So like Stoicism, souls have neither genuine free will nor act by compulsion (*Enn.*IV,3.13). We are free to choose only what our corrupt will

---

[3] A. A. Long and D.N. Sedley, *The Hellenistic Philosophers*, vol. 2 (Cambridge: Cambridge University Press, 1987), 392–3; cf., Epictetus, *Disc.*1.1.7–12.

[4] Margaret E. Reesor, "Fate and Possibility in Early Stoic Philosophy," *Phoenix* 19.4 (1965): 285–297, especially 201.

[5] John Dillon, *The Middle Platonists: A Study of Platonism, 80 B.C. to AD 220* (London: Duckworth, 1977), 166ff.

[6] David Winston, "Chapter 13: Philo of Alexandria" in Lloyd P. Gerson, ed. *The Cambridge History of Philosophy in Late Antiquity* (Cambridge: Cambridge University Press, 2010), 248, footnote 13; The analogies in Philo's *On Providence* are very close to the analogies in Cicero, *De Natura Deorum* II.

determines (borrowed from Stoicism). His view of voluntariness (what we do of our own will) required only that the act was not forced, it was done with knowledge, and that we were *kurioi* (masters) of the act (*Enn*.VI,8.1–4). The later Augustine incorporated all of these Stoic and Neoplatonic theories now taught by Calvinism.

Plotinus also rejected the Jewish and Christian accounts that Adam retained God's image (*imago Dei*) after the fall. He believed humans totally lost the original divine image which could only be regained at physical death (*Enn*.I,1.12; IV,3.12; cf., Augustine's later view). Mimicking Stoicism, a person can only achieve true freedom of will when (by renouncing pleasures and actions) the *autexousion* (self-determination/ power) becomes totally dependent upon the One (Divine Intellect, *Enn*.III, 3.19–21). For Plotinus, Providence controls every miniscule cosmic detail; nevertheless, the One (god) provides limited freedom for some events and persons due to "what depends upon us" made possible *solely* by the indwelling Reason-Principle to produce good (*Enn*.III,3.4-5; III,2.9.1, II,3.1.1). Anything good can only come from the One.

When Neoplatonists were accused of teaching Stoic determinism, they protested and dissented by cleverly limiting "determinism" and "Fate" to astrology, while still teaching Stoic "non-free free will." A totally incapacitating fall from "the One" produces a spiritually dead "evil will" thus requiring the divinely infused gift of love for free choice. The All-Soul (Spirit) gives the gift of love to individuals' souls as the Spirit who implants the desired love (*Enn*.III.5.4). Yet, the One's essential goodness (by definition) exculpates from charge of divine "unfairness" to humans not divinely chosen in Neoplatonic DUPIED.[7] Augustine's later theology incorporated all of these pagan ideas.

---

[7] Long and Sedley (1987), 342, 392.

Space limitations do not permit a summary of my doctoral work analysis of Augustine's Stoic view of the human "evil will" along with his proof-text Latin mistranslations of Prov. 8:35 and Phil. 2:13.[8] But, I am not the first scholar to note Augustine's dependence upon Stoicism. The scholar Byers notes, "Augustine's account of the 'divided self' is deeply indebted to Stoicism."[9] Another scholar summarizes Augustine's later premise drawn from Stoicism and Neoplatonism but without recognizing or acknowledging those sources, "Hence, the good will by which someone begins to will to believe is a divine gift which comes from outside the will."[10]

The covert unilateral determinism of current Augustinian-Calvinism embraces the same types of defenses as Augustine's pagan sources. Augustine followed Plotinus' defense that fate must involve astrology; so, fate from God does not count as fate. The Augustinian scholar TeSelle noted,

---

[8] For example, the five other texts (Ps. 5:12, 68:13, 145:16 [LXX 5:13, 68:14, 144:16]; Sir. 15:15; Lk. 2:14) containing εὐδοκίας refer to *favor, acceptance,* or *good pleasure*, not a "good will" to live righteously in the Stoic sense that Augustine attempted to reinterpret Phil. 2:13 (cf., *gr.et.pecc.or.* 1.6; *ep.* 217.8).

[9] Sara Byers, "Augustine on the 'Divided Self': Platonist or Stoic?" *Aug.Stud.* 38:1 (2007) 105–118.

[10] Marianne Djuth, "Stoicism and Augustine's Doctrine of Human Freedom after 396" in Joseph C. Schnaubelt and Frederick Van Fleteren, eds. *Augustine: Second Founder of the Faith.* Collectanea Augustiniana (New York, NY: Peter Lang, 1990), 387–401.

> Augustine always reacted vigorously to the suggestion that he taught what
> amounted to a doctrine of *fate*. Now it is undeniable that he did hold to some-
> thing like what is usually meant by fate... To him fate meant something pre-
> cise: the doctrine that external occurrences, bodily actions, even thoughts and
> decisions are determined by the position of the heavenly bodies (*C. duat ep
> Pel.,* II,6,12) or more broadly, universal material determinism (*C. duat ep Pel.*
> II, 6,12; *De Civ. Dei.* IV.33, V.1,8).[11]

Augustine admitted if anyone, "calls the will of God or the power of God

itself by the name of fate, let him keep his opinion but correct his language."

(*c.dua.ep.Pel*.1.2.4). Finally, Professor Wolfson, historian and philosopher

at Harvard University's Judaic Studies Center, also concluded Augustine's

"doctrine of grace is only a Christianization of the Stoic doctrine of fate." [12]

C. God Desires All To be Saved

The early church viewed God as relational and responsive to human choices.

The Christian God incorporated foreknown human choices into his prophe-

cies and plans. Wallace accurately identified the earliest Christian leaders

used foreknowledge as their key defense against the Gnostics: "They inter-

preted προορίζω [predestination] as depending upon προγινώσκω (fore-

know)."[13] In contrast to Stoicism's causal nexus, Neoplatonism's One, and

Manichaeism's god, the God of Christianity did not decree everything—de-

spite being sovereign. The first early Christian theologian, Irenaeus (*ca.*185),

---

[11] Eugene TeSelle, *Augustine the Theologian* (New York, NY: Herder and
Herder, 1970; repr. Eugene, OR: Wipf and Stock Publishers, 2002), 313.

[12] Harry Wolfson, *Religious Philosophy: A Group of Essays* (Cambridge, MA:
Belknap Press of Harvard University Press, 1961), 176; Cf., Michael Frede and Hal-
szka Osmolska, *A Free Will: Origins of the Notion in Ancient Thought* (University
of California Press, 2011), especially, "Chapter Nine—Augustine: A Radically New
Notion of a Free Will?"

[13] Dewey Wallace, Jr., s.v. "Free Will and Predestination," in *The Encyclopedia
of Religion*, 2nd edn. (London: MacMillan, 2004).

argued that the Christian God was superior in power to the Gnostic god since he allowed free human choices and could still accomplish his plans (without Stoic divine micromanaging manipulation).[14]

Augustine cites 1 Tim. 2:4—"who desires all men to be saved and to come to the knowledge of the truth"—only once prior to 412 CE (*exp.prop.Rm*.74) and here he uses the traditional Christian understanding. But beginning with his 412 CE departure, he attempts numerous tortured explanations.[15] Finally, in 421 CE (*c.Jul*.4.8.42) Augustine resorted to altering the text to mean "all who are saved." This means those who are saved are only saved by God's will. He repeats this textual change the next year (*ench*.97, 103) wherein "all" means only the elect. People fail to be saved, "not because they do not will it, but because God does not" will their salvation (*ep*.217.19).

D. Conclusion

The early Christian bishops and authors rejected Stoic and Manichaean unilateral determinism (DUPIED) because *Christian* divine foreknowledge

---

[14] Wingren, *Man and the Incarnation*, 3–6. "The essential principle in the concept of freedom appears first in Christ's status as the sovereign Lord, because for Irenaeus man's freedom is, strangely enough, a direct expression of God's omnipotence, so direct in fact, that a diminution of man's freedom automatically involves a corresponding diminution of God's omnipotence." Cf., Irenaeus, *Adv.haer*.II.5.4

[15] Hwang, "Augustine's 1 Tim. 2: 4," 137–42.

was not causal.[16] The essential difference between Christian and pagan philosophy was that the Christian relational God chose persons for salvation based upon his foreknowledge of "future" human choices. These Christians simultaneously taught both God's sovereignty and biblical predestination (God elects by using foreknowledge of genuine human free choice).[17] Their biblical predestination was inextricably connected to divine foreknowledge. Pagan determinism rejected divine foreknowledge because they preferred a non-relational unilateral divine foreordained decree of all future events.

For twenty-five years Augustine defended traditional Christian doctrines against the Gnostic Manichaeans. Yet, he persisted in his meticulous Stoic Providence from his first writings until his death, including the resting position of every leaf and seed being micromanaged (*s.*D29.11). But, he was unable to legitimately transfer Stoic sovereignty into his revised Christianity after 412 CE. So he defaulted to Plotinus' (Neoplatonism's) inscrutability defense (*s.*D.29.10). Augustine appealed to Plotinus' idea of the inscrutable secret counsels of God (the One), who is fair by definition (regardless of the

---

[16] I explain this by analogy of holding a heavy book. I ask the class what will happen if I let go of the book if gravity is not changed and no person intervenes. They reply it will hit the floor. I ask, "Are you 100 percent sure?" They reply "yes." I respond, "So you have perfect foreknowledge?" to which they respond, "Yes." I drop the book. It hits the floor. I look at them and say, "You caused the book to hit the floor." Now they understand why Christian foreknowledge does not cause events. No analogy is perfect, but it makes the point.

[17] For example, Clement and Origen had adapted Stoic concepts and terminology (e.g., προνοία; cf., Acts 24.2) but without succumbing to Stoic determinism. Cf., Van Der Eijk, Ph. „Origines' „Verteidigung des freien Willens in *De Oratione* 6,1-2," *Vig.Chr.*9.1 (2001): 339–351, esp. 347; Jon Ewing, *Clement of Alexandria's Re-interpretation of Divine Providence* (Lewiston, NY: Edwin Mellen Press, 2008), 167–186.

obvious injustice).[18] The Patristics expert Chadwick opined that Augustine was influenced by Platonism far more than even Origen, particularly with sin as privation (e.g., *conf.*7.22).[19] Another scholar concluded, "Condemned through the solidarity of all humans with Adam, they are predestined because God foreknows that he will not give them the grace to be saved. . . . Contrary to the view sometimes expressed, Augustine does speak of the predestination of the damned."[20] In 412 CE, Augustine now embraces a caricature of the Christian God who he syncretized (married) to his Manichaean god. This god will unilaterally damn even innocent infants in a deterministic pagan DUPIED.

Inexplicably, Augustine's Christianized Stoic Providence, which must directly (primarily and actively) micromanage every speck of minutia, somehow miraculously does not sovereignly control evil but only allows/permits it. This view demands that the perfectly holy God who micromanages and decrees everything also decrees evil (in some mysterious and non-culpable manner). This concept comes straight from Stoicism stating that this current world was the best of all possible worlds (cf., the philosophy of Leibniz, *ca.*1710). But if God *only allows/permits* evil then he does not control everything meticulously by decree and thus God is not "sovereign" in the Stoic-Augustinian-Calvinist sense. If God *does* decree evil then he is not the Christian God but the evil creator of matter in Manichaeism (this is then defended by the Neoplatonic appeal to mystery).

---

[18] Hombert dates this to *ca.* April, 412. Cf., *loc.Ex.*20; *s.*294.7.

[19] Henry Chadwick, "Christian Platonism in Origen and Augustine" in Henry Chadwick, ed. *Heresy and Orthodoxy in the Early Church* (Aldershot, UK: Variorum, 1991), 229–30.

[20] Gerard O'Daly, "Predestination and Freedom in Augustine's Ethics" in G. Vesey, ed. *The Philosophy in Christianity* (Cambridge, 1989), 90, (*an.et or.*4.16).

So why does God eternally damn newborn babies? Augustine confessed, "I cannot find a satisfactory and worthy explanation—because I can't find one, not because there isn't one." (s.294.7).[21] No theologian or philosopher in the past 1600 years (since Augustine's reversion to Manichaean determinism) has ever found a satisfactory or worthy answer to this contradiction of a loving Christian God who damns innocent newborns.

---

[21] Translation by Edmund Hill, *Augustine's Works* (Sermon 294), 184.

Chapter 7
Reviewing When and Why Augustine Converted to Determinism

After reviewing the evidence, it appears that Augustine did not follow the apostle Paul's understanding of the New Testament but converted back to his own prior Manichaean interpretations. A summary of this reconversion to determinism will assist us in piecing together his journey.

A. *Ad Simplicianum* in Its Chronological Context

Augustine did not arrive at his later deterministic position in 396/7 CE while writing *Ad Simplicianum* after reading scripture. A systematic, chronological, and comprehensive reading of Augustine's entire corpus exposes his theology as developing in three separate stages. Salvation is based upon: Stage 1.) the foreseen merit of works (386–394 CE), Stage 2.) no foreseen merit of works but only God's foreknowledge of faith alone, per Tichonius (395–411 CE), then finally, Stage 3.) Divine Unilateral Predetermination of Individuals' Eternal Destinies—unilateral election devoid of foreknowledge of even faith (412–430 CE). Scholars often omit Augustine's second stage of traditional election by faith alone, mentioning only divine foreknowledge of good works.[1] Each of these three times Augustine transitions, he breaks quickly

---

[1] Mathijs Lamberigts, "Predestination," in Allan Fitzgerald, ed. *Augustine Through the Ages*: *An Encyclopedia* (Grand Rapids, MI: Eerdmans, 1999), 679.

and decisively from his prior position, completing his theological shift within about one year.

In 412 CE, his final deterministic theology appears simultaneously in his formal works, letters, and sermons. The anomalous *Simpl.* 2.5–22 violates this pattern, about which Wetzel admits:

> As late as the first part of *Ad Simplicianum*, Augustine rests secure in his belief that it remains to a person's free choice to seek the aid of the divine liberator, regardless of how debilitating addiction to sin has become (1.1.14). ... The key elements of Augustine's eventual doctrine of original sin – inheritance of sin (*tradux peccati*) and original guilt (*originalis reatus*) – are already at work here (1.2.20), but it is hard to determine to what extent they dictate his later position.[2]

The reason it is "hard to determine" is because these doctrines immediately and completely disappear for fifteen years. Then suddenly in 412 CE, Augustine laboriously attempts to birth his new deterministic theology, struggling for answers. Few options exist for explaining this disturbing anomaly. The first part of *Ad Simplicianum* (*Simpl.*1) overtly contradicts the latter *Simpl.*2 without any transition. This renders it improbable that he wrote the two parts simultaneously, since Augustine could have revised the letter prior to sending it to Simplicianus.

So how long after 396/7 CE did Augustine revise this letter? When bishop Julian accurately accused Augustine of altering his theology in 418 CE,

---

[2] Wetzel (1999), 798–799; cf., J. Patout Burns, "From Persuasion to Predestination: Augustine on Freedom in Rational Creatures," in Paul Blowers, Angela Russell Christman, David Hunter, and Robin Darling Young, eds. *In Dominico Eloquio, in Lordly Eloquence: Essays on Patristic Exegesis in Honour of Robert Louis Wilken* (Cambridge: Eerdmans, 2002), 307: "In the two decades following his response to Simplician, Augustine generally avoided all discussion of divine control over the will."

Augustine had no answer. This was a fatal problem.[3] Augustine could have used *Simpl.* in its current form to defend himself. He did not. He was too truthful to use a revised work. He may have requested *Simpl.* be returned *ca.*412 CE for revisions, just as he requested that Marcellinus return *Pecc. merit.*1–2 (*ep.*139.3). Can the meager *Simpl.*2.5–22 really hold up to being the only theological "proof" of Augustine's transition for the fifteen years 396–411 CE? Nothing else exists in his twenty-eight major works, and over four thousand letters and sermons from this time period.[4] His traditional Christian theology is taught for another fifteen years. Scholars have missed Augustine's revision of *Ad Simplicianum* about 412 CE. He revised it to match his deterministic conversion. Augustine did not change his theology in 396/7 CE from reading scripture.

When Augustine summarized all of his works in *Retractationes* before his death, he was obligated to creatively defend his pre-412 CE works against multiple accurate accusations that he had previously taught traditional free choice. He reinterprets his pre-412 CE works rhetorically within his new deterministic framework. In describing his works prior to 412 CE, he used extensive "clarifications" to explain how these earlier works "should or could be read" (*ep.*224.2). Note well Augustine's superb professional rhetoric—he does *not* claim how he originally intended them to be read at the time he wrote them, but "should or could be read." Beginning with his works in 412 CE, these strained and imaginative explanatory reconstructions to defend himself suddenly disappear and become unnecessary.

---

[3] Augustine was probably reluctant to cite his revised *Simpl.*2 text in an already published work directly against Julian's allegations that Augustine had changed his theology.

[4] Pope Benedict XVI, *The Fathers of the Church: Catecheses: St. Clement of Rome to St. Augustine of Hippo* (Grand Rapids, MI: Eerdmans, 2009), 150.

But more profoundly, Augustine *never* claims he believed his five major doctrines prior to 412 CE. He truthfully limits himself to grace without merit. This is precisely what he did learn in 394–396 CE by reading works from Hilary of Poitiers, Tichonius, Victorinus, and Jerome on Romans and Galatians. All of these authors taught unmerited grace without works.[5] His carefully crafted phrase in *Praed.*7 suggests a late revision to *Simpl.*2, as "I *began* (*coepi*)" to understand the beginning of faith as God's gift.[6]

By assuming *Simpl.*2 was written in 396 CE, scholars miss Augustine's transition in 395/6 CE from election based upon hidden meritorious deeds to election by unmerited grace (already championed by Victorinus and Tichonius). They assume Augustine's reading of Romans and Galatians evoked his later novel theology.[7] Despite her usual superb insights, Professor Hammond Bammel concluded Rufinus' *Liber de fide* (Book of Faith) was a reaction to Augustine's *Ad Simplicianum* because she assumed *Simpl.*2 dated to 396/7 CE.[8] Therefore, she missed the connection between Augustine's Stoic Providence, damnable *reatus* of original sin, and his deterministic revisionist theology in 412 CE. Rufinus was writing against Manichaeans, not Augustine. The similarity in teachings made it difficult for her and others to distinguish.

---

[5] Daniel Williams, "Justification by Faith: a Patristic Doctrine," *The Journal of Ecclesiastical History* 57 (2006): 649–667.

[6] For a more complete explanation see Wilson, *Augustine's Conversion*, 204–210.

[7] William Babcock, "Augustine and Tyconius: A Study in the Latin Appropriation of Paul," *St.Patr.*17.3 (1982): 1209–1215.

[8] Caroline Hammond Bammel, „Rufinus' Translation of Origen's Commentary on Romans and the Pelagian Controversy," in *Storia ed egesi in Rufino di Concordia*, Altoadriatiche XXXIX (Udine: Arti Grafiche Friulane, 1992), 132–133.

B. Ten Influential Factors

At least ten separate factors significantly influenced Augustine's conversion to Stoic "non-free free will" in his final systematic theology. These are his:

1.) Professional training as a teacher of grammar and rhetoric (not trained in scripture);

2.) Stoic non-relational deterministic Providence derived from Chrysippus and Cicero;

3.) "Full ten years"[9] as a Manichaean learning to reinterpret Christian and Jewish scriptures in the Manichaean deterministic sense;

4.) Neoplatonic philosophical conversion in Milan through the Christian bishop Ambrose, which opened the door to Augustine's Christian conversion;

5.) Preoccupation with sexual sin, renouncing his sexual intercourse with several concubines by vowing permanent chastity to achieve salvation;

6.) Illegal appointment as bishop of Hippo (no co-bishoprics were allowed yet he held a co-bishopric with the older Valerius) that was almost blocked by his primate (archbishop) Megalius' accusations of Augustine's Manichaean sympathies;

7.) Excellent intellect and ability to synthesize various religions and philosophies;

8.) *Hubris* (arrogance) to consider his own Christianized Stoic Providence (unilateral determinism) correct and every prior Christian

---

[9] Henry Chadwick, *Augustine: A Very Short Introduction.* (Oxford: Oxford University Press, 1986), 14; James O'Donnell, *Augustine: A New Biography* (New Yok, NY: Harper Collins, 2005), 45, says a minimum of eleven years; cf. p.48, "he fudges the count."

author for 300 years wrong about humanity's residual traditional free
choice to receive God's gift of salvation;

9.) Polemical personality as he combated multiple different heresies;

10.)North African origin with its strong local tradition of practicing infant
baptism.

Some of these factors considered separately were not unusual. Both Cyprian
and Tertullian resided in North Africa as rhetoricians. Origen, the Cappado-
cians, Victorinus, and Ambrose were influenced by Neoplatonism. Others
such as Epiphanius conveyed a polemical personality combating heresies.
Origen at least equaled Augustine in intellectual and synthesizing abilities,
if not surpassing him. Yet all of these prior authors remained within traditional free choice theology.

The literature lacks any prior prominent Christian bishop or author who
had spent a decade with a concubine and fathered a child, then obtained another concubine awaiting his arranged marriage.[10] Roman law prevented
marriage between certain classes resulting in the commonplace of concubi-
nage (a common-law marriage). Augustine berates himself excessively for
this relationship. Even his oft-quoted "so give what you command, and then
command whatever you will" usually omits the prior part of the sentence,
"In this respect too you lay upon us the injunction to continence [no sexual
relations]" (*Conf.*10.60). A Christian bishop or author who renounced these
sexual relationships for chastity as a "salvific" experience proves unprecedented. He was preoccupied with physical sexual sin from his Manichaean
background and incorporated a sexual inheritance of damnation at birth (inherited guilt) into his doctrine.

---

[10] Cf., François Decret, *Early Christianity in North Africa* (*Le christianisme en
Afrique du Nord Ancienne*), trans. by Edward Smither (Cambridge: James Clarke
and Co., 2011), 163; and, Chadwick (1986), 16.

Vicious rhetorical arguments were common enough in ancient Christian writings. For example, Optatus' berating of Donatus (*ca.*385)[11] stated Donatus set himself up almost as God (3.3; *ca.*385). But nowhere else do we find rhetoric so extreme from polemical zeal as Augustine's defamation in claiming the Christian Donatists were anti-Christs, damned Christians. He claimed they equated Donatus with God; and, that "some" of them did not believe Jesus to be equal to the Father, and some denied that Christ had come in the flesh (*s.*183). Stroumsa noted this vicious tactic excluded Christian Donatists from the Church universal through a "far-fetched biblical exegesis" of 1 John 2:2.[12] In the end, Augustine's compulsive polemicizing rhetoric gutted his exegetical accuracy. In addition, his capacity to synthesize Stoicism, Neoplatonism, Manichaeism, and Christianity surpassed even Mani's intentionally syncretic religion of Manichaeism.

The following three factors figure most prominently in explaining Augustine's later conversion to determinism: infant baptism, Stoicism, and Manichaeism. Augustine's deterministic conversion would not have occurred without the infant baptismal tradition in his local North Africa. Only in North Africa and nearby Rome do we have the earliest proofs for infant baptism, and only with Augustine does a newborn's salvation from inherited eternal damnation come by proxy through parental faith. This claim was challenged by a contemporary local bishop. Prior to 412 CE, even Augustine had viewed baptism as unnecessary for salvation and infant baptism had no explanation. Therefore, as Sage concluded, speculating an apostolic origin

---

[11] Mark Edwards, *Optatus: Against the Donatists* (Liverpool: University Press, 1997), xviii.

[12] Gedaliahu Stroumsa, "*Caro salutis cardo*: Shaping the Person in Early Christian Thought," *History of Religions* 30 (1990): 45.

for infant baptism to forgive damnable guilt inherited from Adam appears unlikely.[13]

Clement and Origen had adapted and Christianized many Stoic concepts and terminology (e.g., πρόνοια; cf. Acts 24:2) but without succumbing to Stoic determinism.[14] No Christian bishop or author before Augustine had so extensively imbibed the Stoic Providence of Chrysippus and Cicero.[15] Similarly, embracing the pagan philosophical "evil will" (Stoic, Ciceronian, and Neoplatonic) and his mistranslation of Prov. 8:35 allowed an explanation for sin in the "dead will" not found in Paul's Romans 7 or any other scripture.[16] Augustine's Stoic "non-free free will," totalitarian Providence, Epictetus' "evil will," and Plotinus' "dead will" were unparalleled influences. While earlier Christians exalted God's general sovereignty, this did not entail a Stoic dictatorial micromanagement of every event in the universe, although

---

[13] Sage, "Le péché original dans la pensée de saint Augustin, de 412 à 430," *REAug* 13 (1969): 75–112.

[14] Philip van der Eijk, „Origines' Verteidigung des freien Willens in *De Oratione* 6,1–2," *Vig.Chr.* 9.1 (2001): 347; Jon Ewing, *Clement of Alexandria's Reinterpretation of Divine Providence* (Lewiston, NY: Edwin Mellen Press, 2008), 167–186.

[15] Robert O'Connell, *Augustine's Early Theory of Man* (Ann Arbor, MI: Belknap Press of Harvard University Press, 1968), 189, regarding *c.Acad.*1.1 and *Sol.*1. Although overstating Augustine's dependence upon Plotinus and Porphyry in some areas [cf. Bonner (1984), 495–514; Dodaro and Lawless (2000); Ayres (2010), 13–41], O'Connell rightly identifies this Stoic/Neoplatonic influence for Augustine's view of Providence; cf. Ronald Tanner, "Stoic Influence on the Logic of St. Gregory of Nyssa," *St.Patr.*18.3 (1989): 557–584.

[16] Serge Ruzer, "The Seat of Sin in Early Jewish and Christian Sources," in Jan Assmann and Guy Stroumsa, eds. *Transformations of the Inner Self in Ancient Religions* (Leiden: Brill, 1999), 367–391. Paul could not do the good he willed.

they recognized God's intermittent direct engagement (minimal specific sovereignty) within history.

Similarly, no known prior Christian author had spent a decade as a Manichaean believing Divine Unilateral Predetermination of Individuals' Eternal Destinies (unilateral determinism/fate). Early church policy prohibited prior Manichaeans from becoming bishops due to this dangerous doctrine. This almost prevented Augustine's ordination and remained an issue raised by his opponents even prior to the Pelagian controversy. This is probably why Augustine wrote *Confessions*. His ordination as co-bishop with Valerius was illegal, forbidden by the Nicene Council. These illegal exceptions provided Augustine with his platform for leadership. The Manichaean hymn of the dead soul/will being unilaterally raised by infused faith through Christ's radical grace still reverberated in his memory decades later. This Manichaean radical grace had already been expounded by Basilides two centuries prior as God's gift in Gnostic determinism and refuted by Clement. The early church's policy of prohibiting prior Manichaeans from becoming bishops had been wise.

After reconverting to determinism, Augustine redefined numerous terms such as predestination, original sin, grace, free will, etc. Weaver concluded that Augustine had "considerably altered" his definition of free will (cf. *Praed.*8).[17] Augustine's transformation of Christian predestination into Gnostic/Manichaean unilateral determinism produced valid objections from the catholics of his age. Nevertheless, his redefinitions persist into modernity as many scholars still confuse Christian predestination (election to eternal

---

[17] Rebecca Weaver, "Anthropology: Pelagius and Augustine on Sin, Grace, and Predestination," in Everett Ferguson, Frederick W. Norris, Michael P. McHugh, eds. *Encyclopedia of Early Christianity*, 2nd edn. (New York, NY: Garland Publishing, 1999), 63.

salvation based upon foreknowledge) with Augustinian "predestination" (more accurately labeled DUPIED, fate, or pagan determinism).[18]

Finally, in stark contrast to Augustine's causal determinism (DUPIED), the last Greek church father, John of Damascus (d.*ca.*760), retained traditional Christian predestination (divine election based on foreknowledge): "We ought to understand that while God knows all things beforehand, yet He does not predetermine all things. ... So that predetermination is the work of the divine command based on foreknowledge." (*Exp. fid.*44).

C. Converting the Cause and Date of Augustine's Conversion to Determinism

In this work, I have challenged four foundational assertions that are accepted pervasively within Augustinian studies:

1.) Augustine changed his theology in 396 CE
2.) while he was writing the letter to Bishop Simplicianus (*Simpl.*),
3.) with his transition occurring through studying scripture (Romans 7, Romans 9, and 1 Corinthians 15),
4.) which he developed through merely modifying prevalent doctrines.

This chronological and comprehensive analysis of Augustine's massive number of works, and comparison with earlier authors, challenges these claims

---

[18] Ralph Mathisen, "For Specialists Only: The Reception of Augustine and His Teachings in Fifth-Century Gaul," in Joseph Lienhard, Earl Muller, and Roland Teske, eds. *Augustine: Presbyter Factus Sum* (New York, NY: Peter Lang, 1993), 30–31; Eugene TeSelle, *Augustine* (Nashville, TN: Abingdon Press, 2006), 81.

made by prior scholars.[19] Only in 412 CE, while writing *Pecc. merit.*, were Augustine's embryonic ideas conceived, birthing them in *Spir. et litt.*, and then developing perseverance as a gift from God a decade later. By his own admission, the essential foundations of his innovative system were (his mistranslated proof-texts of) Rom. 5:12 and Prov. 8:35, and the African tradition of infant baptism.[20] Even Valentinian, the primate (archbishop) of neighboring Numidia, wrote to Augustine questioning his novel view of infant baptism (*ep.*5*).

After writing fifty-five (extant) books, Augustine's first full citation of Rom. 5:12 in a treatise, to support inherited guilt from Adam, occurs only in 412 CE (*Pecc. merit.*). Citations of Romans 7, Romans 9, and 1 Corinthians 15 were frequent prior, but only after 411 CE do their reinterpretations rest upon his Rom. 5:12 foundation. Traditional original sin had been embraced for three centuries, with Melito rivaling Augustine in emphasizing human depravity.[21] However, the Bishop of Hippo did not merely modify, but erased three centuries of teachings on traditional original sin and free choice by adding his damnable inherited *reatus* (Augustinian original sin with

---

[19] Wetzel (1999), 798–799; Brown, P. (2000), 147–148; Ernest Evans, *Tertullian's Homily on Baptism* (London: SPCK, 1964), 101; Gregory Ganssle, "The development of Augustine's view of the freedom of the will (386–97)," *Modern Schoolman* 74 (1996): 1–18; Rigby (1999), 607–614; Harrison, C. (2006); Virgilio Pacioni, "Providence," in Allan Fitzgerald, ed. *Augustine Through the Ages: An Encyclopedia* (Grand Rapids, MI: Eerdmans, 1999), 686–688; Charles Warren, *Original Sin Explained?: Revelations from Human Genetic Science* (Lanham, MD: University Press of America, 2002).

[20] Jean Laporte, "From Impure Blood to Original Sin," *St.Patr.*31 (1997): 438–444 at 443, indicating the limited geographical scope.

[21] Even if this is credited to rhetorical effect during a homily, it remains impressive.

damnable guilt). Building upon one scholar's claim, Augustine was not merely "the architect of the theology of original sin,"[22] but a contractor who demolished the foundation of Christian free will to construct a contradictory theology built on pagan fate and Manichaean determinism.[23]

Simultaneously, Augustine's traditional free choice became Stoic "non-free free will" via the "evil willer/chooser" of Epictetus and Plotinus. Chrysippus had cleverly redefined causal determinism to separate it from necessity (fate) by inventing a counterfactual possibility of opportunity that was impossible to achieve. This means even though the person had zero possibility of actually using that opportunity, (some type of) "free will" remained (*Fat.*12–15).[24] Having read Chrysippus (through Cicero), Augustine knew this highly nuanced pagan position of pseudocompatibilism.[25] But prior Christian authors had rejected as heresy every pagan, Gnostic, or Manichaean anthropology with total inability to respond to God. This total

---

[22] Julius von Gross, *Entstehungspeschichte der Erbsündendogmas*, Bd.1 (München: Ernst Reinhardt, 1960), 368.

[23] Contra Pier Beatrice, *Tradux Peccati. Alle fonti della dottrina agostiniana del peccato Originale* in Studia Patristica Mediolanensia 8 (Milan: Vitae Pensiero, 1978), 35: Inherited damnable *reatus* was not "gia vitale e circolante in ambienti ecclesiastici italiani o africani," (already vital and circulating in the ecclesiastical environment in Italy or Africa) and he inexplicably dismisses Manichaeism as the source for Augustinian original sin (p.67).

[24] Long and Sedley (1987), vol.1, 393.

[25] Pseudocompatibilism is thinking human genuine freedom of choice and absolute divine determinism can co-exist simultaneously, although it requires clever manipulations like the Stoics used. This is a false concept invented by the Stoics to salvage their declining popularity with the common people. This ploy is still used in modern discussions to defend "compatibilism."

inability required a divine "gift of faith by grace" and necessitated a unilateral fated choice by a false god or the Fates.

This was no mere modification—Augustine "sovereignly" rejected one of the most foundational doctrines held universally by early Christians.[26] Sovereignly designed order (meticulous providential micromanagement) remained a critical element in Augustine's philosophy, and it should be crucial to scholars as the Bishop of Hippo's massive corpus is interpreted. One reason that excellent scholars have overlooked Augustine's final conversion in 412 CE results from neglecting Augustine's advice: "For whoever reads my works in the order in which they were written will perhaps discover out how I have made progress over the course of my writing." (*Retract.,* Prol.3).

The evidence demonstrates Augustine did *not* convert from traditional Christian free choice to "non-free free will" in 396 CE while writing *Ad Simplicianum* as a result of studying scripture (Romans and 1 Corinthians), by merely enriching earlier Christian ideas. Scholars have only assumed this from Augustine's vague comments as a professional rhetorician that (like modern politicians) can be understood in different ways. Scholars have not recognized his revisions of *Lib. arb.*3.47–54 and *Simpl.*2. None of his final major doctrines studied are detectable from 396–411 CE. These only appear in 412 CE when he overreacts to the extreme when fighting the Pelagians.

But the one doctrine Augustine consistently taught from his youth until his death was Stoic Providence. Because his Stoic Providence ordained *everything*, he re-interpreted the church tradition of infant baptism by using the mistranslated Rom. 5:12 and Prov. 8:35 as his self-admitted foundational

---

[26] Contra Charles Baumgartner, "Théologie dogmatique," *RecSR.*51.4 (1963): 623 and *Le Péché originel* (Paris: Desclée, 1969), Baumgartner's claim that Augustine merely verbalized what the church implicitly believed does not match the evidence.

arguments. With these he replaced Christianity's *regula fidei* (rule of faith) of traditional free choice with Stoic "non-free free will" and pagan unilateral determinism. The great Augustine underwent numerous conversions in his personal journey—Stoicism, Manichaeism, Neoplatonism, Christianity with works meriting grace, Christianity with unmerited grace, and then Christianized Manichaean radicalized grace.[27]

D. Augustine Stands Alone Against the Early Church

Early Christian authors unanimously taught *relational* eternal predetermination. God elected persons according to his foreknowledge of their faith (predestination). This Christian stand opposed Stoic Providence and Gnostic/Manichaean unilateral determinism (fate).[28] While they were teaching predestination, Christians refuted Divine Unilateral Predetermination of Individuals' Eternal Destinies (DUPIED).[29] This determinism is first identified in ancient Iranian religion, then chronologically in the Qumranites, Gnosticism, Neoplatonism, and Manichaeism. Heretics such as Basilides, who taught God unilaterally bestowed the gift of faith, were condemned. Of the eighty-four pre-Augustinian authors studied from 95–430 CE, over fifty authors addressed the topic. All of these early Christian authors championed traditional free choice against pagan and heretical Divine Unilateral

---

[27] Harrison is correct about Augustine's continuity in grace but she does not recognize it is radical Manichaean grace, not Christian grace. See Carol Harrison, *Rethinking Augustine's Early Theology: An Argument for Continuity* (Oxford: Oxford University Press, 2006).

[28] Sarah Stroumsa and G. Stroumsa (1988): 48.

[29] Wallace was previously cited and refuted on pg. 19. The early church fathers prior to Augustine taught predestination, not Stoic fatalism and Manichaean determinism.

Predetermination of Individuals' Eternal Destinies (see Wilson, *Augustine's Conversion,* Appendix III, pages 307–9 and the Timeline Chart on Determinism and Free Choice at the end of this book).

Like Athanasius, the great defender of the Nicene faith, (*C. Ar.*2.75–77), all pre-Augustinian Christian authors understood Eph. 1:4, "just as He called us before the foundation of the world" as only proper to a God whose foreknowledge affected Providential election.[30] "Foreknowledge" of future free choice explained God electing persons to eternal life.[31] These early Christian authors concurred with Cicero's *De fato* 11.27–28 solution—God's knowledge is restricted to cognition, not causation.[32] But unlike Cicero, early Christians retained God's infallible, omniscient foreknowledge. This *regula fidei* (rule of faith) of traditional free choice may be a rare example of genuine unanimity throughout Christendom in the early centuries.

As early as *ca.*120 CE, Christian authors had advocated physical death and a corrupted human nature from Adam's fall (*Barn.*) while acknowledging a residual free choice (*Herm.*). This persists until 412 CE when Augustine converts to his later theology. Contrary to some persons' assertions, bishops in the eastern Mediterranean region were not biased to support Pelagius due to a "lesser view" of original sin. Some modern authors alleged a Greek-Latin/East-West dichotomy on original sin. They claimed Eastern bishops rejected it and Western bishops accepted it. But this cannot be confirmed

---

[30] Alvyn Pettersen, *Athanasius (*London: Geoffrey Chapman, 1995), 30–36.

[31] Appropriately viewed by Augustine as "atemporal" (or better 'omnitemporal') and thus an anthropomorphism. If God lives simultaneously in the past, present, and future, then foreknowledge only applies from a human perspective.

[32] Barry David, "The Meaning and Usage of 'Divine Foreknowledge' in Augustine's *De libero arbitrio (lib. arb.)* 3.2.14–4.41," *AugStud* 32.2 (2001): 117–156.

with facts.[33] Rather, the Eastern bishops' and Cyril's reaction are accurately explained in this way:

> in its earliest years, the reactions to Pelagianism were occurring principally in the East. [...] Cyril's theology about the difference between nature and grace, the inheritance of original sin, the inclination towards sin, and the necessity of grace all accord with Augustine's opinions.[34]

E. Conclusion

Therefore, it was Eastern bishops, not Augustine, who initiated the fight against Pelagianism. Augustine's unique and extreme reaction to Pelagianism began in 412 CE, and moved him into unknown territory for Christians. He added damnable guilt to original sin and demanded radical Manichaean grace to awaken a dead soul by divinely infused faith. Not one author prior to Augustine taught humans were born damned thereby requiring God first to alter a person's fallen nature by regenerating him or her with faith and grace before that individual could respond to God.

All prior authors taught God had already provided grace to all helpless humans in the person of Christ. Humans only needed to accept God's gift of salvation in Christ through their own residual God-given divine image (i.e., free choice). Augustine's writings prior to 412 CE also embrace this traditional free choice theology. After 411 CE, Augustine stood all alone in his pagan deterministic view of Divine Unilateral Predetermination of Individuals'

---

[33] Otto Wermelinger, *Röm und Pelagius: die theologische position der römischen Bischöfe im pelagianischen Streit in den Jahren 411–432* (Päpste und Papsttum VII; Stuttgart: Hiersemann, 1975), 263–278; Wermelinger exemplifies the typical misrepresentation of „Die Lehreinheit zwischen Ost und West" on original sin.

[34] Geoffrey Dunn, "Augustine, Cyril of Alexandria, and the Pelagian Controversy," *AugStud* 37.1 (2006): 63–88. He cites Jerome's *Ep.*19 and Cyril's first work (*De adoratione in spiritu et veritate*).

Eternal Destinies (DUPIED). Later, his disciples joined him.

Conclusion

We have investigated the changes Augustine made to Christianity with his novel theology. Although applauded for his anti-Pelagian works, his views on divine determinism were not generally accepted until the Protestant Reformation. Why was this the turning point?

A. The Protestant Reformation

The originator of the Protestant Reformation, Martin Luther, was an Augustinian monk who revived Augustine's pagan deterministic theology. In 1525 CE, he wrote against the work, *Free Will* by Erasmus of Rotterdam by publishing his own work *De servo arbitrio* (*On the Bondage of the Will*).[1] Luther accepted Augustine's view of Stoic sovereignty and the Manichaean view of total inability to respond to God. Luther went to the extreme in arguing against Catholic abuses by trying to make everything in salvation be of God without any human works. Augustine had changed faith into a work. So for Luther, even initial faith had to be God's gift.

John Calvin was influenced by Stoicism and wrote his first book on the Stoic philosopher Seneca's *De Clementia* at the age of twenty-four. He did not accept all of Stoicism's ideas and rejected neostoicism, but did hold the

---

[1] Although orthodox regarding Christian doctrine, Erasmus believed practical righteousness of the Christian was more important than nit-picking orthodoxy.

Stoic view of sovereignty.[2] Calvin's successor, Theodore Beza, wrote regarding Seneca: "This very grave writer being obviously in accordance with Calvin's disposition, was a great favourite with him."[3] Calvin was drawn to Augustine through that common Stoic commitment because a God who micromanages everything fit his philosophy.[4] Calvin quotes Augustine over 400 times in his *Institutes of the Christian Religion*. He admitted, "Augustine is so wholly within me that I could write my entire theology out of his writings."[5]

Augustine was the inventor of the five points of Calvinism. His five points of total inability, unconditional election, limited atonement (propitiation), "irresistible" grace, and perseverance are the five points of Calvinism. This is why Helm, as a Calvinist, advocates the term "Augustinian-Calvinism."[6]

In the final eighteen years of his life, Augustine taught pagan divine unilateral determinism—the opposite theology of every prior Christian author and the opposite of Augustine's own earlier doctrine. The elder Augustine used the very same deterministic scriptures he had learned in Manichaeism,

---

[2] Ford L. Battles, "Sources of Calvin's Seneca Commentary," in *Interpreting John Calvin* (Grand Rapids, MI: Baker, 1996), Chapter 2 and Appendix C.

[3] Theodore Beza, *"The Life of John Calvin" in Tracts Relating to the Reformation* by John Calvin, vol. I; trans. by Henry Beveridge (Edinburgh: Calvin Translation Society, 1956), 24.

[4] John Sellars, *Stoicism* (Bucks, UK: Acumen, 2006), 142.

[5] John Calvin, "A Treatise on the Eternal Predestination of God," in John Calvin, *Calvin's Calvinism*, trans. Henry Cole (London: Sovereign Grace Union; repr., 1927), 38. Calvin in his *Institutes* quotes Augustine many hundreds of times.

[6] Paul Helm, "The Augustinian-Calvinist View" in James Bielby and Paul Eddy, eds. *Divine Foreknowledge: Four Views* (Downers Grove, IL: IVP), 161–189.

and taught Manichaean interpretations he (and all other Christian authors) had previously refuted as heresy.[7]

Both Luther and Calvin mistakenly believed that Augustine was merely teaching what all of the earlier church fathers who preceded him had taught.[8] How could this happen? Augustine consistently utilized the same Christian terms as prior authors but inserted his own new meanings into those terms. In doing this, he exchanged his traditional Christian doctrine for pagan philosophies and Manichaean interpretations of scripture.[9] Luther and Calvin

---

[7] For a list of these scriptures used by Manichaeans to prove their unilateral determinism, used by the elder Augustine, and now currently used by Reformed theologians, see Wilson, *Augustine's Conversion*, 371.

[8] Calvin did recognize Augustine went far beyond the earlier authors by adding total depravity, teaching humanity had a dead "willer." *Inst.* II.2.4.

[9] This includes the terms original sin, grace, predestination, free will, etc. See Andre Dubarle, *The Biblical Doctrine of Original Sin* (London: Geoffrey Chapman, 1964), 53: "For example, in the early patristic writers we find references to the *origin of sin*, to a *fall*, and to the *inheritance of sin*, but what is meant is often different from the meaning given to those terms in the later classical tradition influenced by Augustine"; Ralph Mathisen, "For Specialists Only" 30–31; Rebecca Weaver, s.v. "Predestination," in *Encyclopedia of Early Christianity*, 2nd edn., Everett Ferguson, ed. (New York, NY: Garland Publishing, 1998): "The now centuries-old characterization of the human being as capable of free choice and thus accountable at the last judgment had been retained, but the meaning of its elements had been considerably altered"; Peter Leitheri, "Review of *Adam, Eve, and the Serpent* by Elaine Pagels," *Westminster Theological Seminary Journal* 51.1 (Spring, 1989), 186: "Augustine's concept of free will certainly differs from that of earlier theologians"; Cf., Wilson, *Augustine's Conversion*.

were misled by Augustine.[10] Augustine claimed that he was teaching what all of the earlier church fathers were teaching. This is partially true compared to the Pelagians "omitting grace" but not at all true about his unilateral determinism versus free choice of every prior author. So Augustine changed the meaning of free will from a Christian to a Stoic definition. The human will was free only to choose sin so "the evil will" could not respond to God. Augustine used the words ("free will") but altered the meaning.

Luther and Calvin were not the only ones misled. After the Protestant Reformation in 1738 a Baptist pastor named John Gill was trying to prove Calvinism was an ancient idea. Gill attempted to enlist the early church fathers before Augustine as teaching TULIP by taking quotes from pre-Augustinian authors out of context.[11] Some modern Calvinist authors use Gill's list

---

[10] Martin Luther, "Letter to Spalatin" (October 19, 1516) and *Lecture on Romans*, Glosses and Scholia, Chapter 4 in *Luther's Works*, vol. 48, Letters I, J. Pelikan, H. Oswald, and H. Lehmann, eds. (Philadelphia, PA: Fortress Press, 1999); John Calvin, *Institutes of the Christian Religion* I.xiii.29; Wolfson, *Religious Philosophy*, 158–76 in which he explains the centuries-old traditional Jewish and Christian understanding of free will (despite the sinful inclination) that persisted until the "later Augustine" introduced Stoic ideas into Christian theology, and especially Augustine's misunderstanding of *concupiscentia* in his Latin translation of *Wisdom of Solomon* 8:21.

[11] John Gill's *The Cause of God and Truth* in 1738 claimed the early church taught TULIP. He uses his own mistranslations of ancient texts, ignores context, and assumes without warrant that words like "elect" and "predestination" carry the meanings Augustine inserted into them (redefinitions accepted by modern Calvinists). I am unaware of even one Patristics scholar who would agree with these unfounded and illegitimate claims.

of quotes without realizing his errors.[12]

B. Inspecting the Foundation of Augustinian-Calvinism

Augustinian-Calvinists claim the only person to correctly interpret the apostle Paul's deterministic scriptures for the first four centuries was Augustine. But of course, they omit the Stoics, Gnostics, and Manichaeans who previously interpreted these texts as teaching unilateral determinism. Somehow, Calvinists purport only Augustine—baptized in highly deterministic Stoicism, Neoplatonism, and Gnostic-Manichaeism—got it right. In their view, every one of over fifty early church fathers got it wrong on human freedom of choice. Even Augustine himself admitted that he had tried but failed to continue in the essential and unanimous Christian doctrine of free will throughout the first four centuries: "In the solution of this question I

---

[12] For modern Calvinists repeating his errors see Michael Horton, *Putting Amazing Back into Grace* (Nashville, TN: Thomas Nelson, 1991), Appendix 219–241 [note the revised and updated 2011 edition omits all of these citations]; and, Dr. C. Matthew McMahon's website for "Calvinism in the Early Church" accessed on 7-20-2019 at https://www.apuritansmind.com/arminianism/calvinism-in-the-early-church-the-doctrines-of-grace-taught-by-the-early-church-fathers/. Both authors seem unaware of the scholarly research that overwhelmingly proves the contrary (much of which was collated and published in my recent book *Augustine's Conversion*). McMahon is at least correct about Prosper of Aquitaine and Fulgentius of Ruspe who were the two most ardent disciples of Augustine. No pre-Augustinian Christian author taught TULIP. For a podcast summary of these Calvinist errors when citing early Christian authors please consult my second discussion with Dr. Leighton Flowers on "Soteriology 101" from July 31, 2019 at https://youtu.be/YTSEh1o8HdE.

struggled in behalf of free choice of the will, but the grace of God won out."[13]

The famous Reformed theologian Benjamin Warfield commented, "The Reformation, inwardly considered, was just the ultimate triumph of Augustine's doctrine of grace."[14] Warfield's statement is pinpoint accurate. But unfortunately, due to Luther's and Calvin's reliance upon Augustine, the unmerited grace of the Christian God did not triumph. In Augustinian-Calvinism (Reformed) theology, it was the radicalized grace of the Manichaean god that triumphed.

Augustine was the father of TULIP: Total depravity (total inability to respond to God), Unconditional election (Stoic/Gnostic/Manichaean DUPIED), Limited atonement (Christ only died for the elect), Irresistible grace (violent Manichaean grace), and the gift of Perseverance (invented by Augustine to explain the extreme differences in how persons lived their lives following salvific infant baptism). Therefore, modern Calvinism in these deterministic distinctives has more in common with ancient philosophies and religious heresies than with early Christianity. An objective evaluation of the facts cannot avoid this startling conclusion.

Because current Calvinist deterministic interpretations of scripture passages are interpretations brought into Christianity through Augustine's Manichaean past, Calvinism is built upon the teachings of ancient *Manichaeism*. Calvinism leans upon *Manichaean* interpretations of key scriptures. Calvinism lacks a solid historical and biblical foundation within early Christianity. It rests upon unstable sand of ancient heretical and pagan doctrines. For these

---

[13] Augustine, *Retr.*2.1. Even Augustine recognized pseudocompatibilism was not an option. Human free choice and absolute (Stoic) specific sovereignty cannot co-exist.

[14] Benjamin Warfield, *Calvin and Augustine* (Philadelphia, PA: Presbyterian and Reformed Publishing, 1956), 332.

reasons, the tiny foundation upholding the impressively logical structure of Augustinian-Calvinism should be pronounced unstable and condemned as unsafe.

C. Alternatives to Augustinian-Calvinism

There are alternatives. The theologies of every other major branch of Christianity—Roman Catholicism, Eastern Orthodoxy, and all other Protestants—are built upon the solid foundation of the unanimous Christian free choice perspective taught for over three centuries before Augustine. The sovereign God of *Christianity* graciously offers salvation to every human equally (not creating some people for the purpose of damning them eternally for his glory). And, because every human retains God's image, every human retains the capacity for a free choice response to God's grace for salvation. (This did not require God to infuse faith to awaken the Manichaean dead soul.) God's election of persons is based upon his foreknowledge of human choices. (Christian election does not follow Gnostic teaching of the unilateral elect and damned based on Stoic eternal decrees controlling every detail in the universe.) Christ died for every human being (not solely for the elect).[15] All other major branches of Christianity stand firmly with the early church in these teachings against pagan Stoic, Gnostic, Neoplatonic, and Manichaean divine unilateral determinism.

Early Christianity taught GRACE: **G**od offers salvation equally, **R**esidual free choice response, **A**tonement universally, **C**onditional election based on foreknowledge, and **E**ternal life for those who respond in faith. These concepts comprise the solid GRACE foundation championed by earliest Christianity over against heretical and pagan deterministic DUPIED and the later Augustine's TULIP. The Christian God of love sacrificially invited all humans to join him in eternal life.

---

[15] Authors do differ in understanding how the early church viewed the atonement. See David Allen, *The Extent of the Atonement: A Historical and Critical Review* (Nashville, TN: B & H Academic, 2016). I disagree with Allen on his treatment of Augustine and Prosper but support his argument for Origen, Athanasius, Cyril, Ambrose, Chrysostom, and other early church fathers who taught that Christ's death was both sufficient to redeem and intended for every human being. That is, Christ did not die only for the elect. These early authors made clear faith was required for Christ's sacrifice to be efficacious such that only the elect were redeemed (contra universalism). The question of limited efficacy was not debated until after Augustine's conversion to determinism when he altered his theology by teaching God did NOT desire every individual human to be saved; because, God created many persons for the purpose of eternally damning them for the praise of his glory.

Appendix 1
"I've always been a Calvinist: What do I do now?"

If you are a Calvinist, this book should not cause you to abandon your faith. Apostasy from Calvinism does not mean you are not one of the elect. It does mean you value truth over tradition. Augustine is rightly a father of the Roman Catholic Church and respected as a philosopher in western civilization. Augustine still held firmly to the essentials of Christianity. But that does not mean everything he taught was correct. The Roman Catholic Church does not teach Augustine's determinism. One should appreciate Augustine for his contributions to Christianity while recognizing he stepped out of bounds when fighting the Pelagians.

If you understand the pagan sources of Augustine's conversion to determinism, you should consider leaving Augustinian-Calvinism. Augustine was the only Christian bishop in history known to have been heavily influenced as a young man by participating in the three most highly deterministic systems that have ever existed—Gnostic Manichaeism, Neoplatonism, and Stoicism. Augustine's deterministic ideas did not come from the apostle Paul (a Pharisee who believed in free choice). Over fifty earlier Christian authors fought against those fated philosophies by teaching free choice. This new knowledge of how and why Augustine moved back into pagan determinism should greatly concern us. When these facts are combined with the knowledge that both Luther and Calvin mistakenly believed Augustine was merely teaching what all the earliest church fathers taught, Augustinian-Calvinism is exposed as built upon an unstable foundation of pagan sand.

Beginning with "God is sovereign" is not a Christian, but a Stoic foundation of philosophical theology.[1] All other major Christian groups outside of Calvinism hold forth as primary what I believe to be a more important element of theology: "God is love." We should choose to love the God who first loved ALL of humanity (every human equally) and we should choose to love the humanity that God loves.

Every religion and every philosophy has difficulties and problems. None are perfect. Every human, including me, makes mistakes. Keep this book handy when you read "deterministic" passages so you can see how early Christians interpreted them instead of how Gnostics and Manichaeans misinterpreted them. Their pagan god was non-relational. Instead, embrace a loving Christian God who invites you to choose, not a pagan god who hypnotizes you to change your mind.[2]

---

[1] See my forthcoming book in 2020, *God's Sovereignty: An Historical, Philosophical, and Theological Analysis.*

[2] For more information on free will, I recommend Tim Mawson, *Free Will: A Guide for the Perplexed* (London: The Continuum International Publishing Group, 2011).

Deterministic Philosophies
of Pagans and Augustine

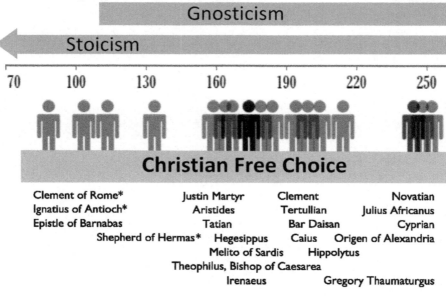

Gnosticism

Stoicism

| 70 | 100 | 130 | 160 | 190 | 220 | 250 |

Christian Free Choice

Clement of Rome*   Justin Martyr   Clement   Novatian
Ignatius of Antioch*   Aristides   Tertullian   Julius Africanus
Epistle of Barnabas   Tatian   Bar Daisan   Cyprian
        Shepherd of Hermas*   Hegesippus   Caius   Origen of Alexandria
                         Melito of Sardis   Hippolytus
                    Theophilus, Bishop of Caesarea
                              Irenaeus   Gregory Thaumaturgus

Unanimous Free Choice of Early
Christianity (Rejected Determinism)

* Three of the earliest of the fifty-three merely suggest Free Choice

Neoplatonism

Manichaeism

Augustine

| 280 | 310 | 340 | 370 | 400 | 430 |

Methodius of Olympus
Arnobius of Sicca
Lactantius

Hegemonius/Pseudo-Hegemonius
Maximus, Bishop of Jerusalem
Eusebius of Caesarea

Hilary of Poitiers
Epiphanius of Salamis
Ephrem the Syrian
Marcellus of Ancyra
Gregory Nazianzen
Basil of Caesarea
Ambrosiaster
Gregory Nyssen
Gaius Marius Victorinus
Athanasius
Tichonius
Pseudo-Macarius
Cyril of Jerusalem
Nemesius of Emesa
Macarius of Egypt
Diodore of Tarsus
Rufinus of Syria
Ambrose of Milan
Didymus the Blind

Jerome
Pelagius
Theophilus of Alexandria
Theodore of Mopsuestia
John Cassian
John Chrysostom
Rufinus of Aquiliea

Made in the USA
Las Vegas, NV
14 April 2021

21385746R00079